FLOWERS
COLORING BOOK

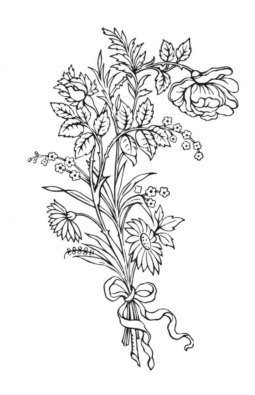

FLOWERS
COLORING BOOK

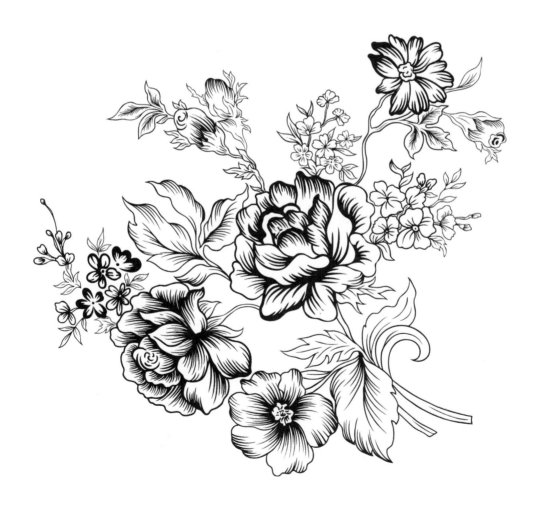

CHARTWELL
BOOKS

This edition published in 2013 by
CHARTWELL BOOKS
an imprint of Book Sales
a division of Quarto Publishing Group USA Inc.
142 West 36th Street, 4th Floor
New York, New York 10018

ISBN: 978-0-7858-3041-2

AD003566NT

Printed in China
Reprinted in 2013, 2014, 2015 (four times).

INTRODUCTION

Use the outlines in this book to produce your own beautiful flower artworks and patterns with colored pencils.

Think carefully about your color scheme and try to give the images either a harmonious or contrast-strong combination of colors. Remember to think about color tone – this can make the difference between a vivid, strong picture and a subtle, pale picture.

Pencil color is not as intense as paint, so it really helps to add layers. When using darker shades, don't just apply one layer of color. Darker tones look better if you work over the same area several times to produce a greater intensity of color. For example, most black areas are either warm or cool in hue. To achieve this, apply a layer of black and then add another layer of deep brown or dark blue on top. If you want to make the black even more intense, put blue over brown over black, or brown over blue over black. Then, for the really dense areas, add another layer of black.

When making blue or red, add layers of different blues and reds to increase the intensity. Sometimes the addition of purple can also give a blue or a dark red more power in the composition. Other times, your top layer can be put on quite lightly, just to change the quality of the color a little.

Try making the tonal marks of the pencils in different directions – cross-hatching, zigzagging or spiraling – to give your finished artwork an interesting texture.

Happy coloring!

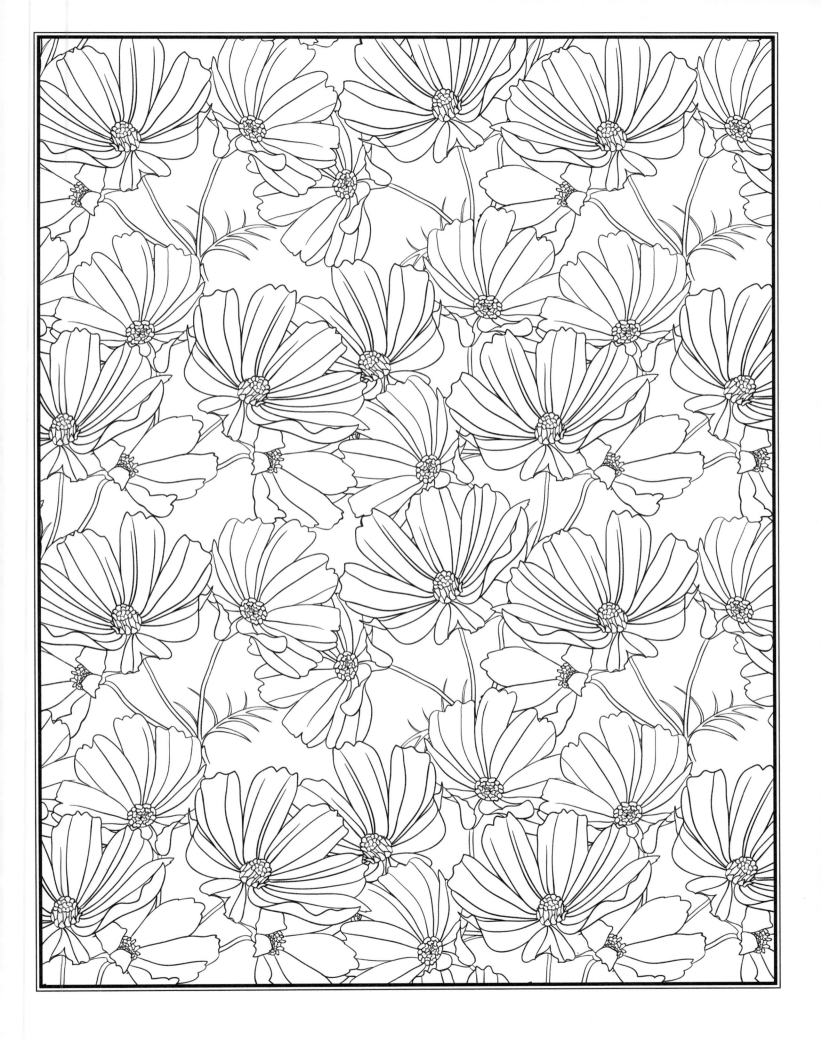

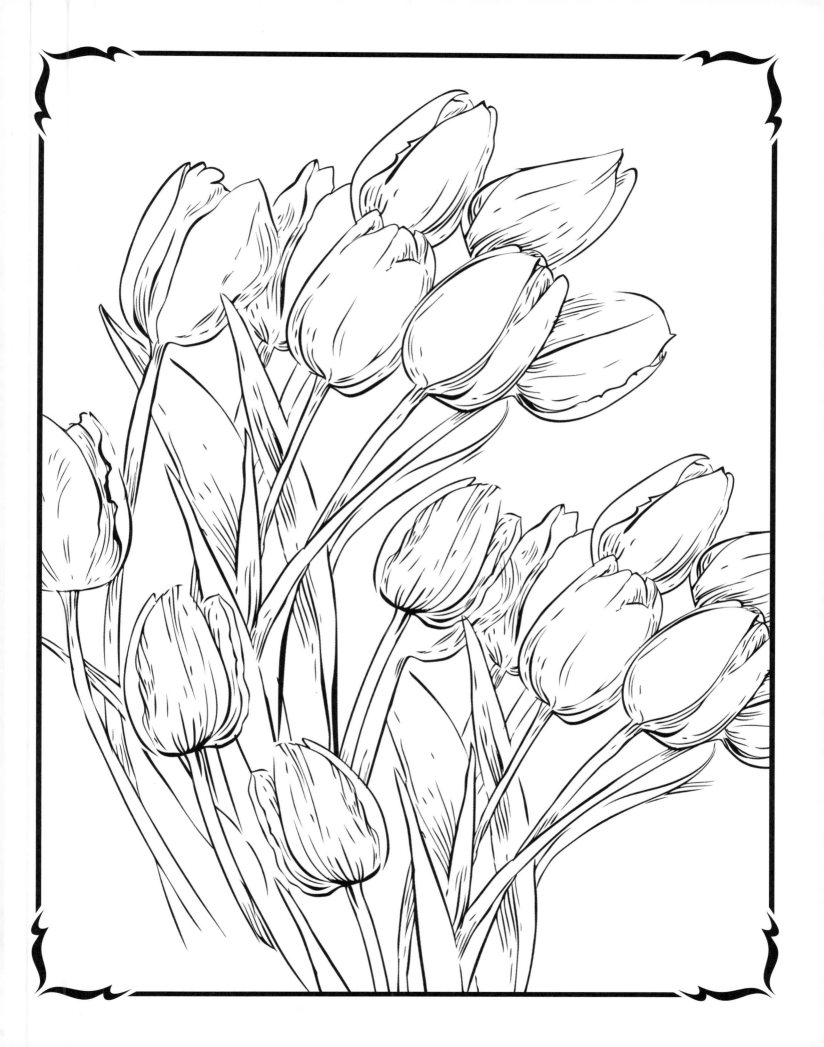

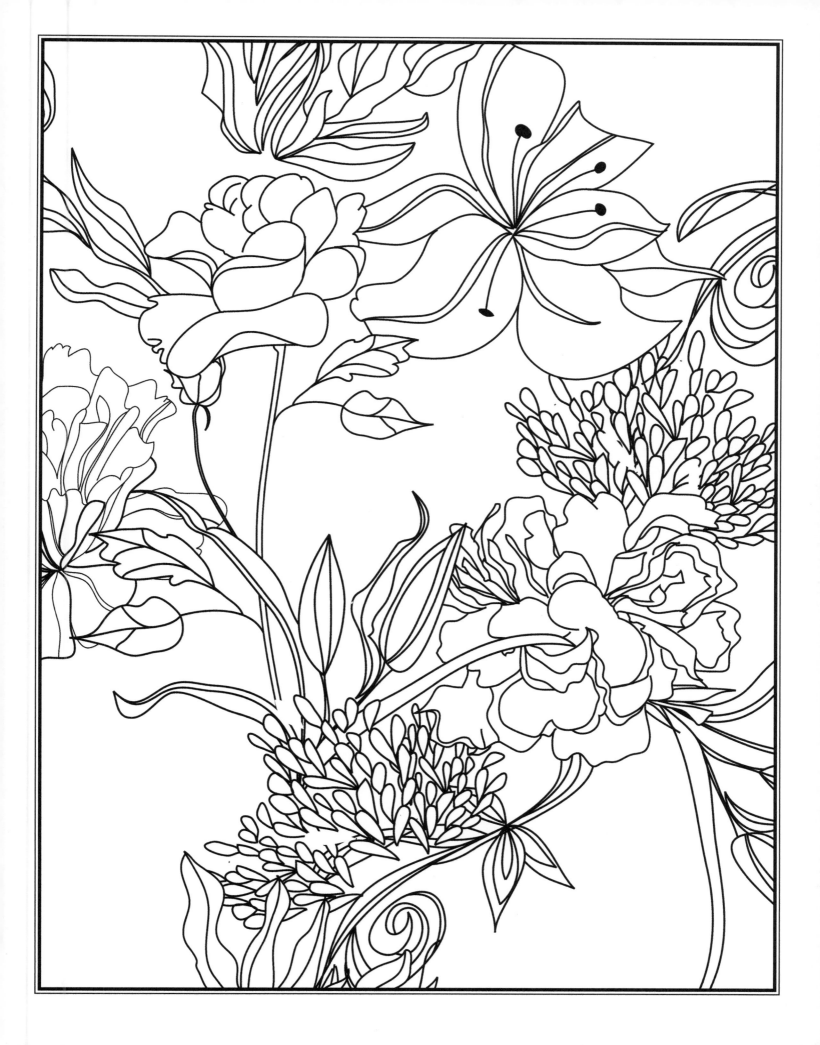

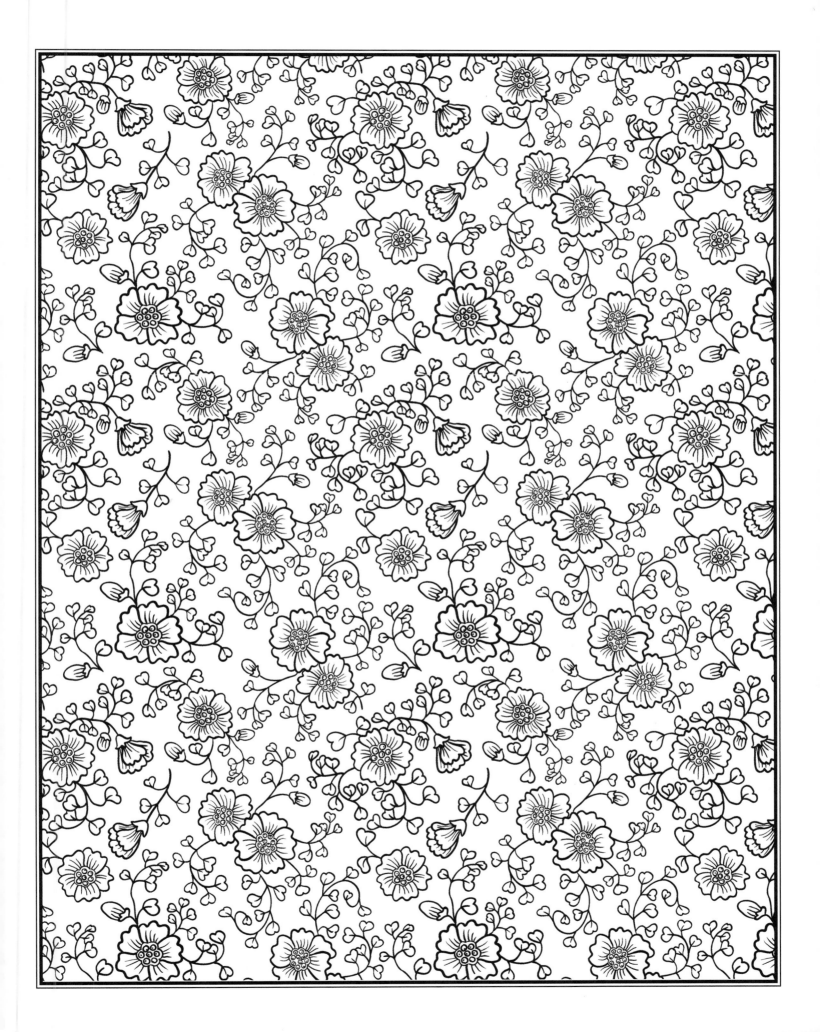

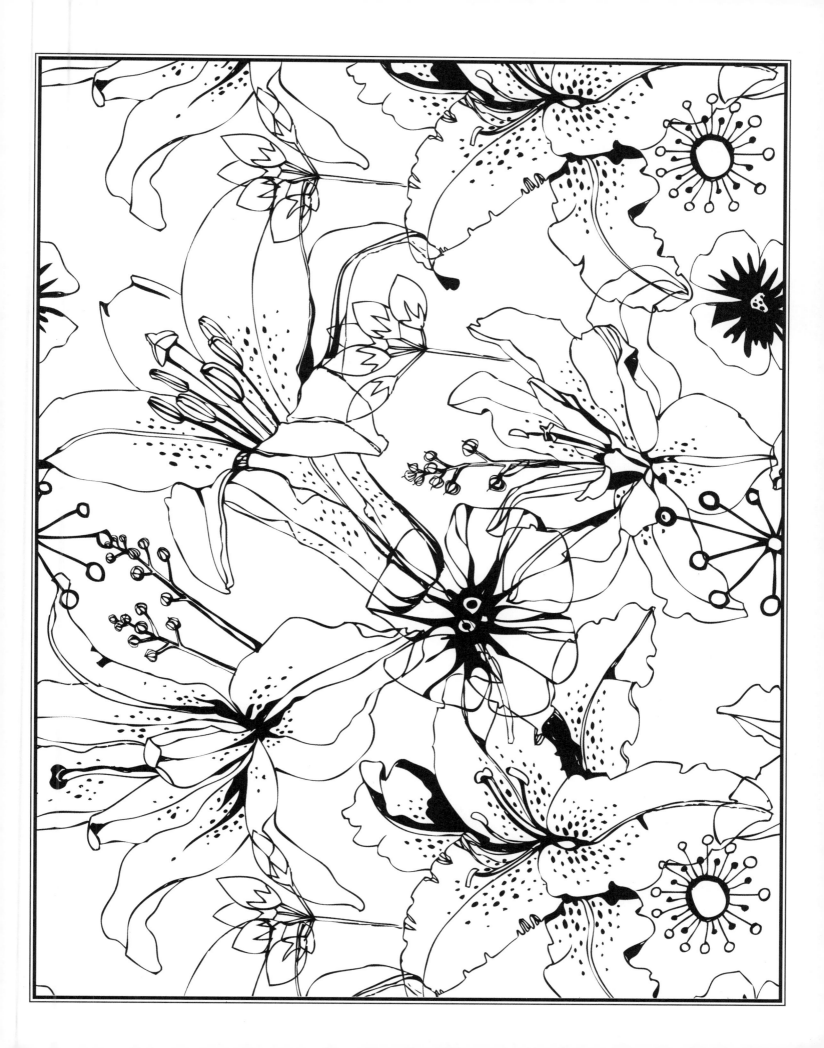

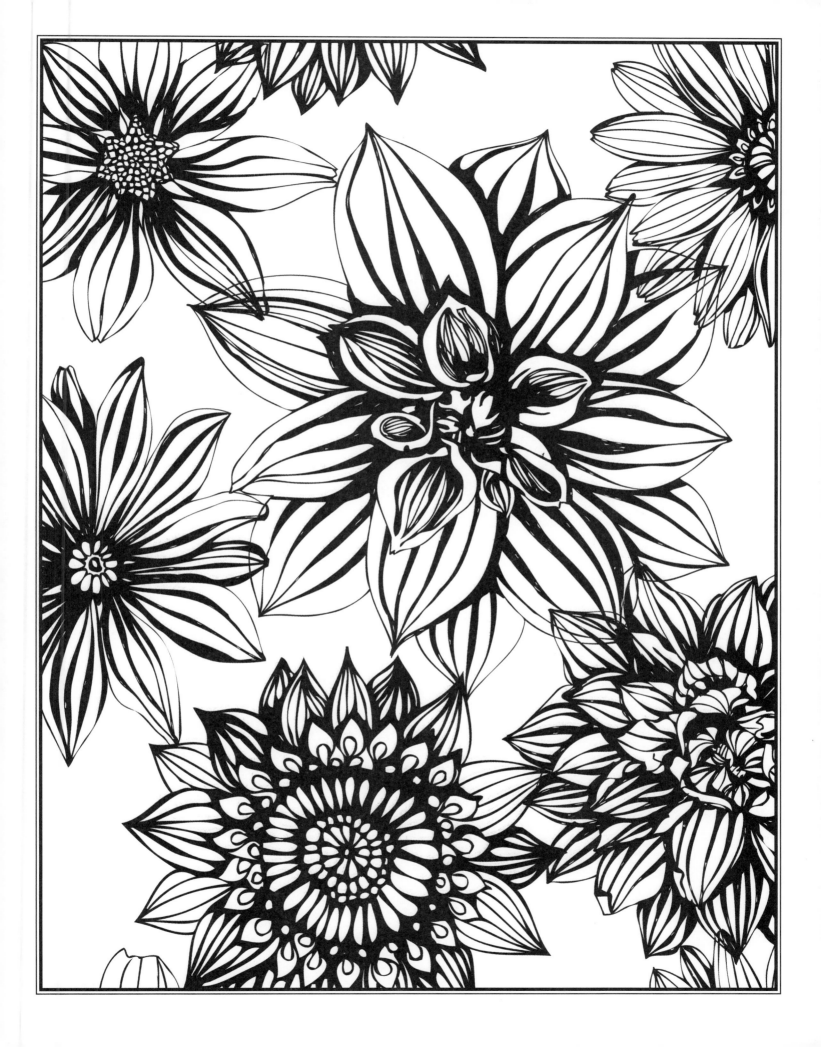

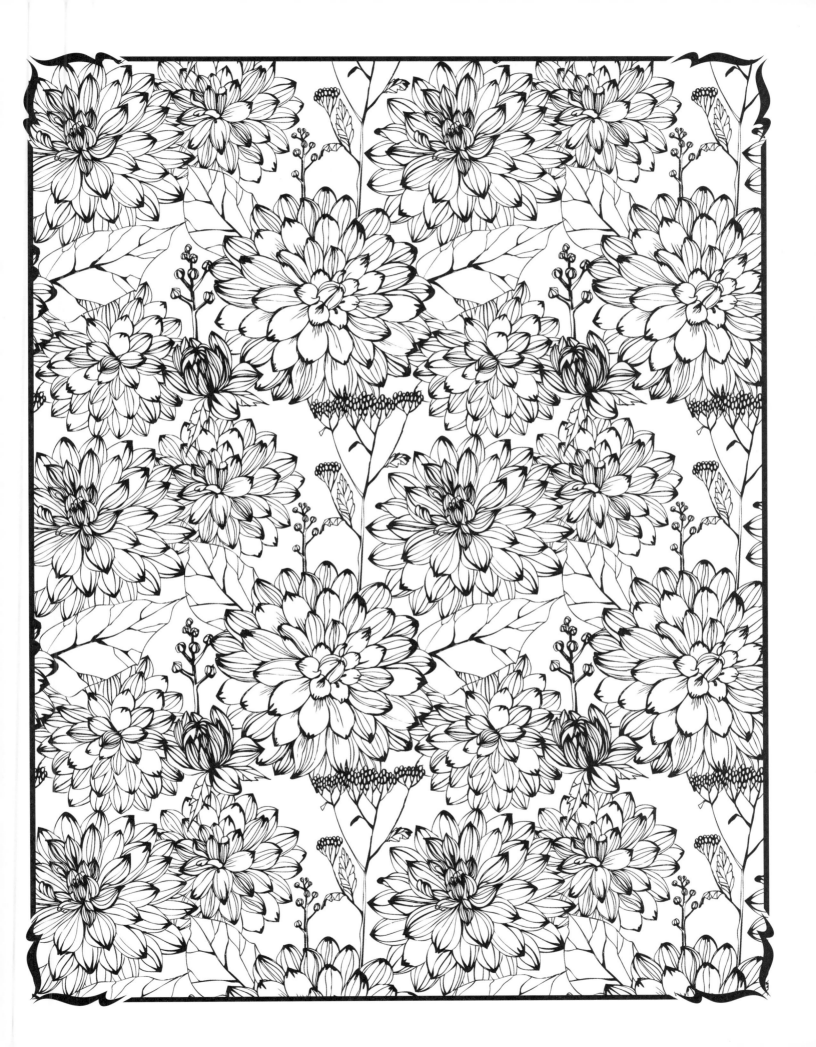

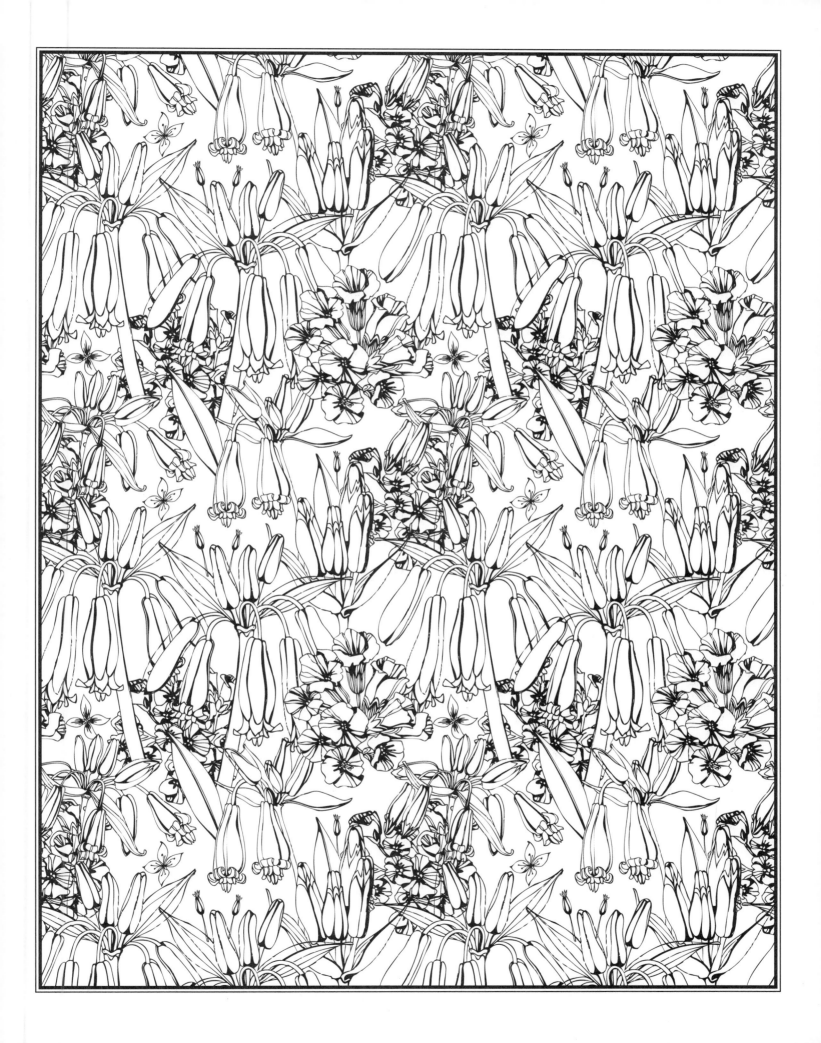

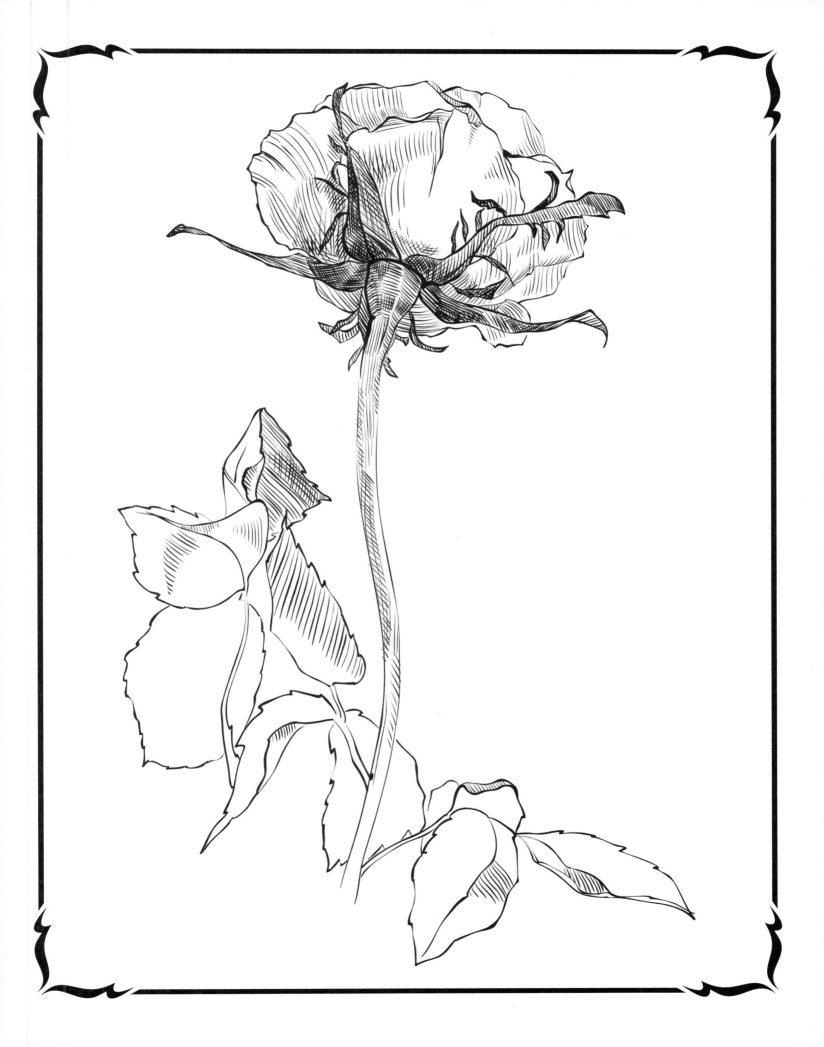

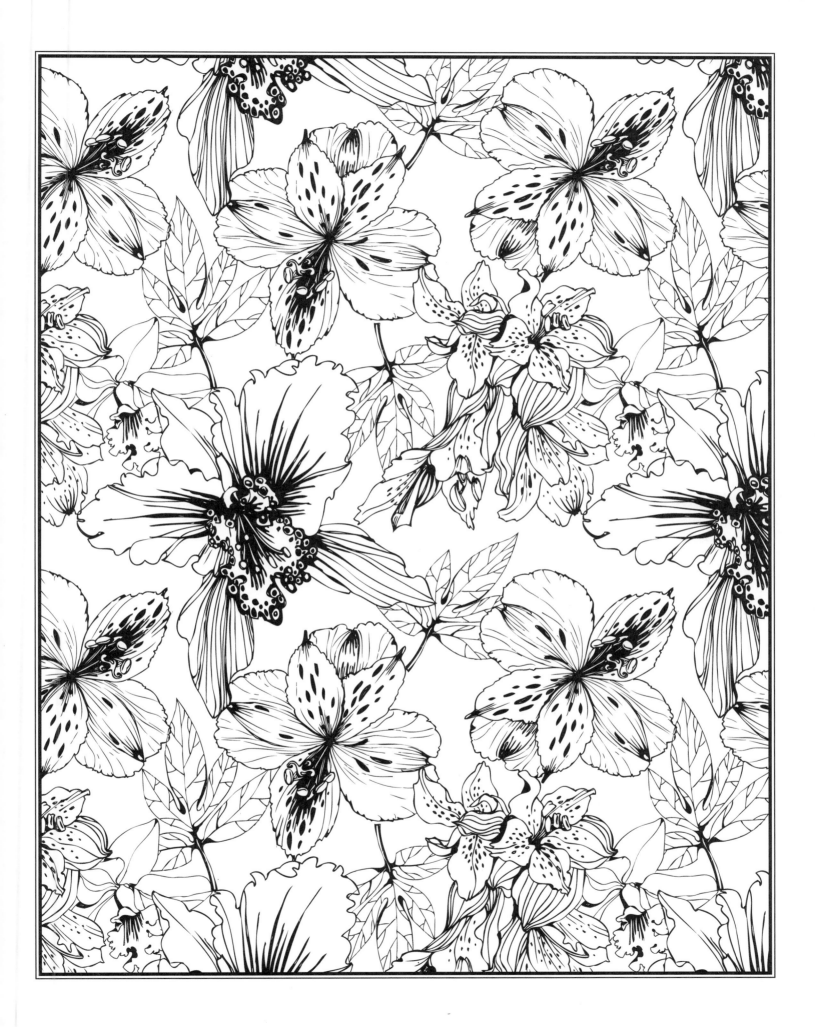

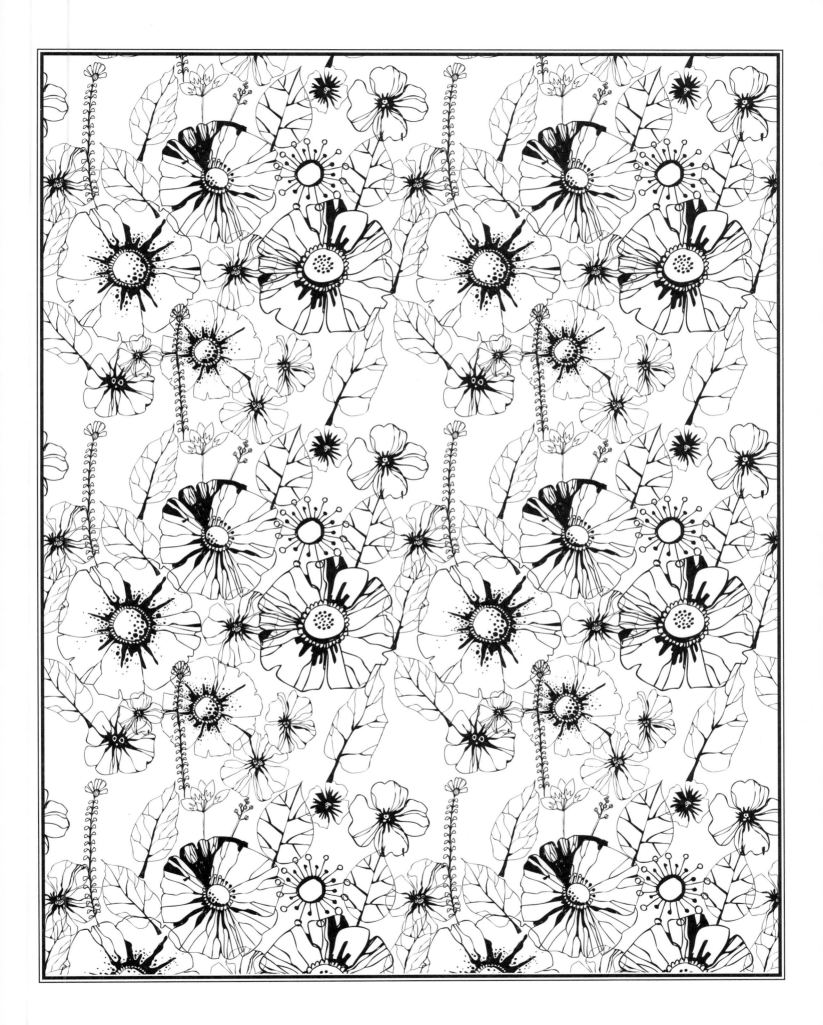

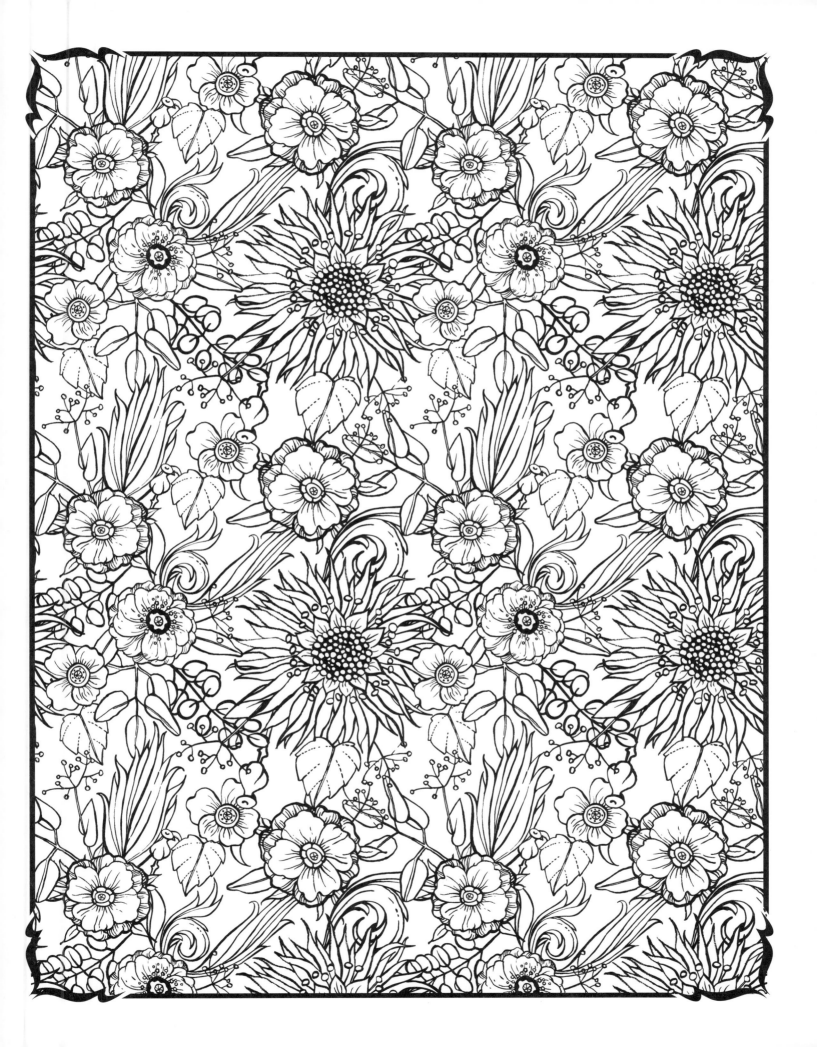

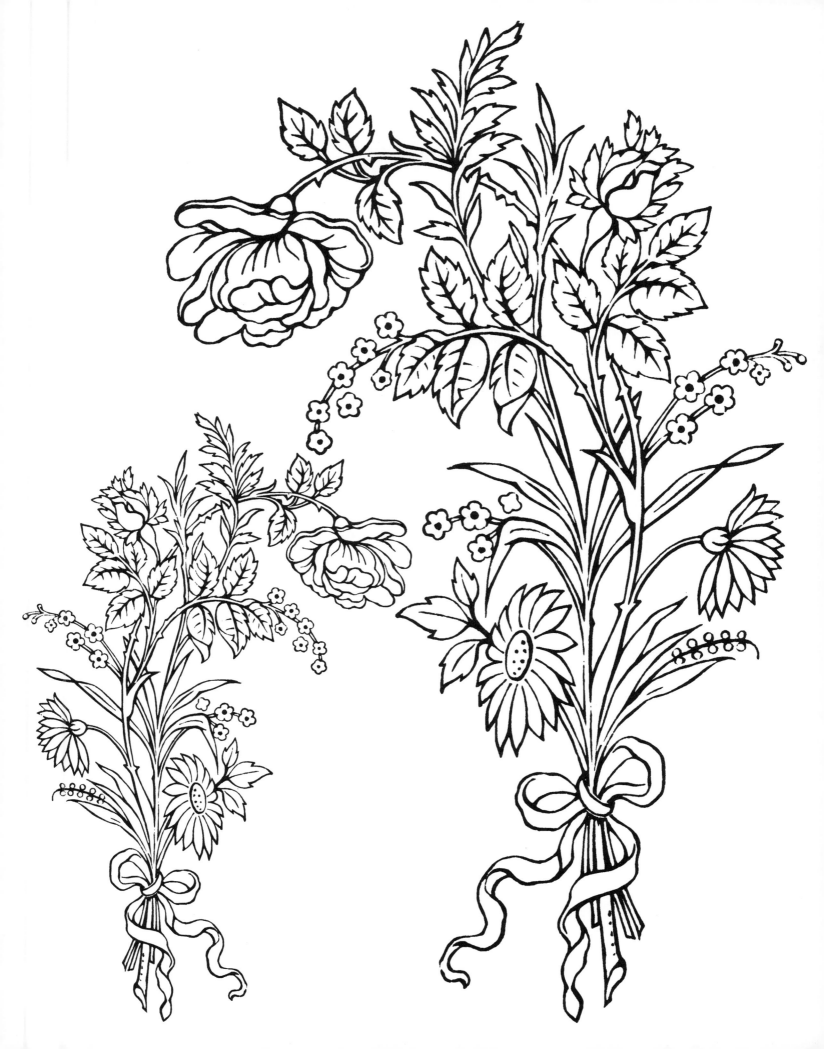

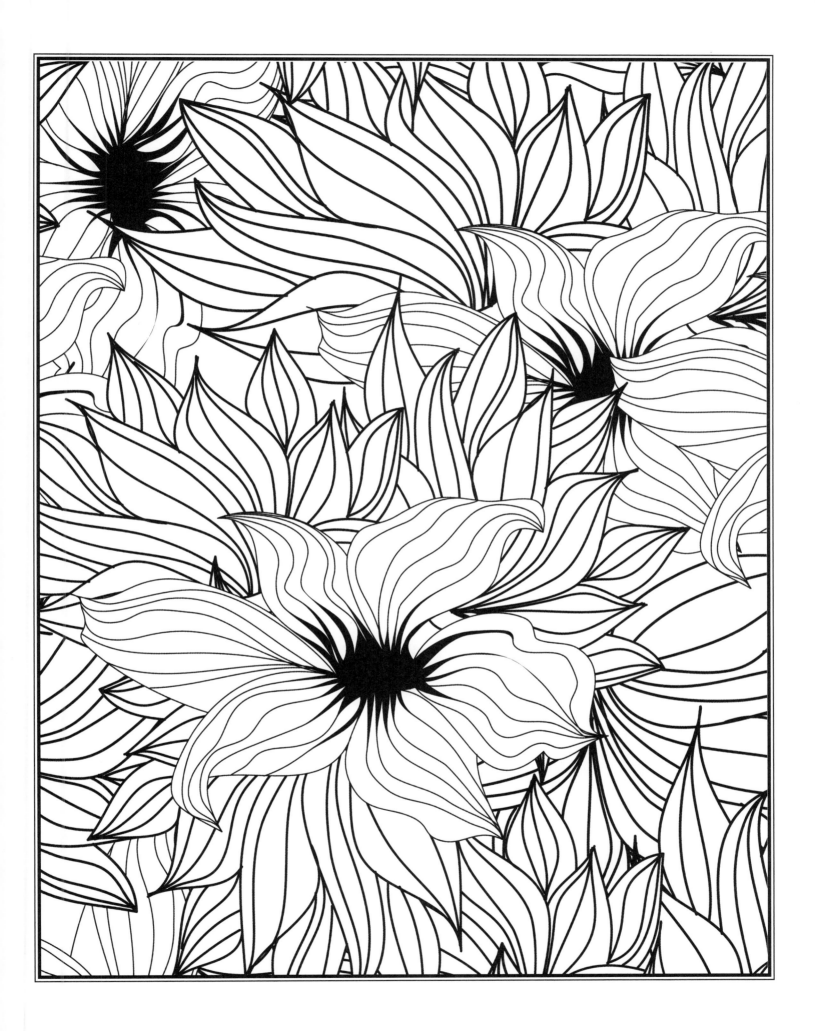

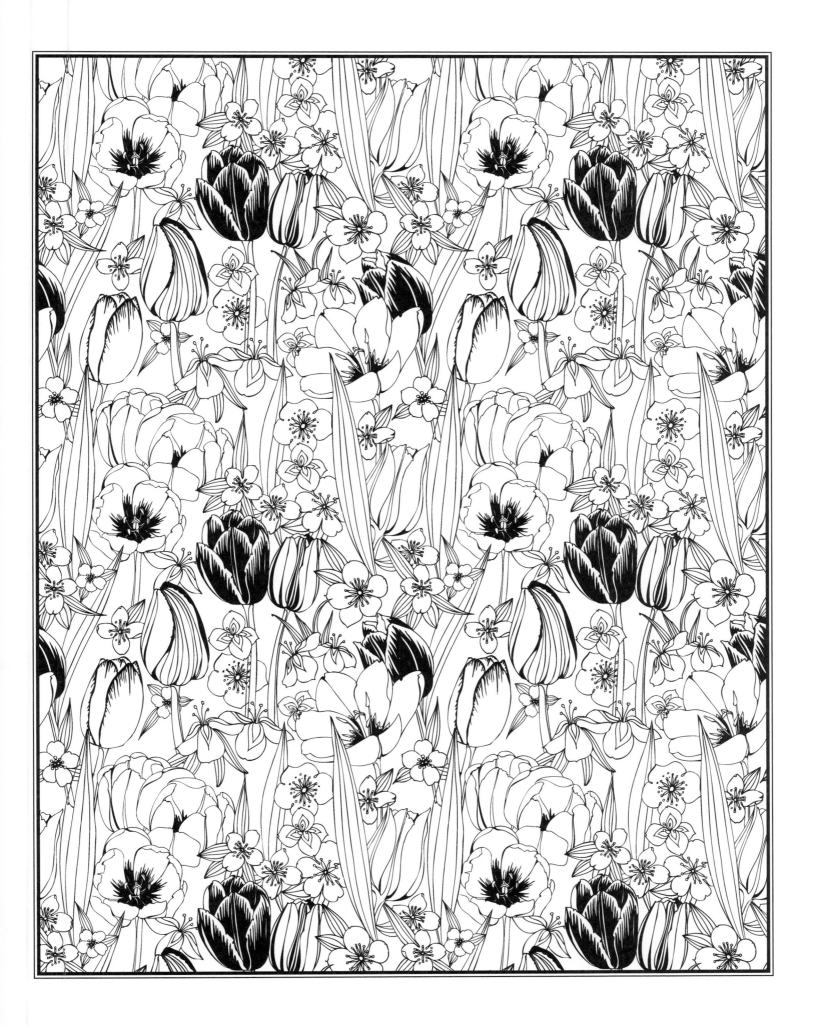

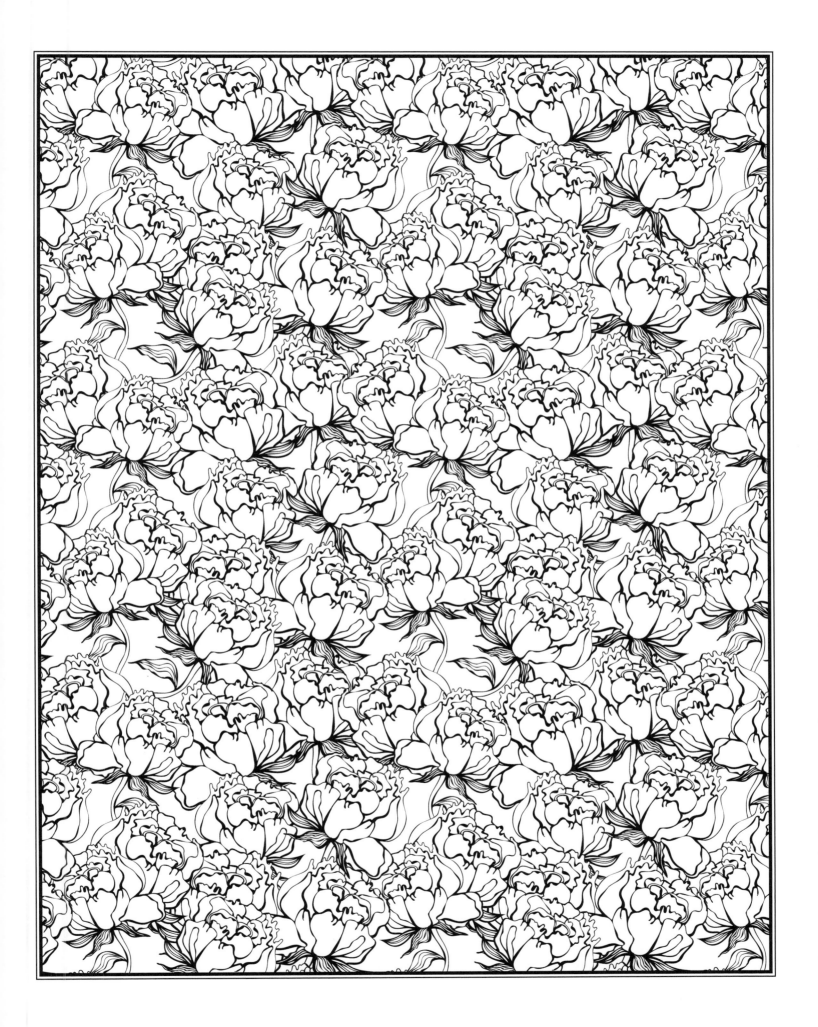

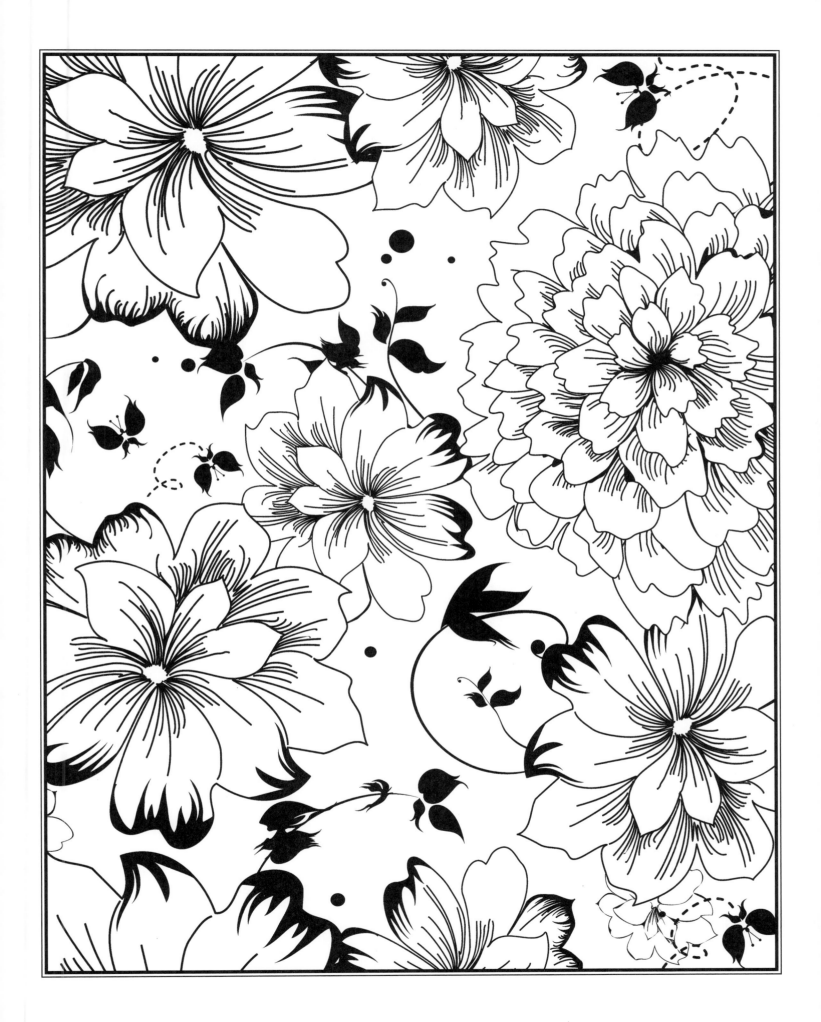

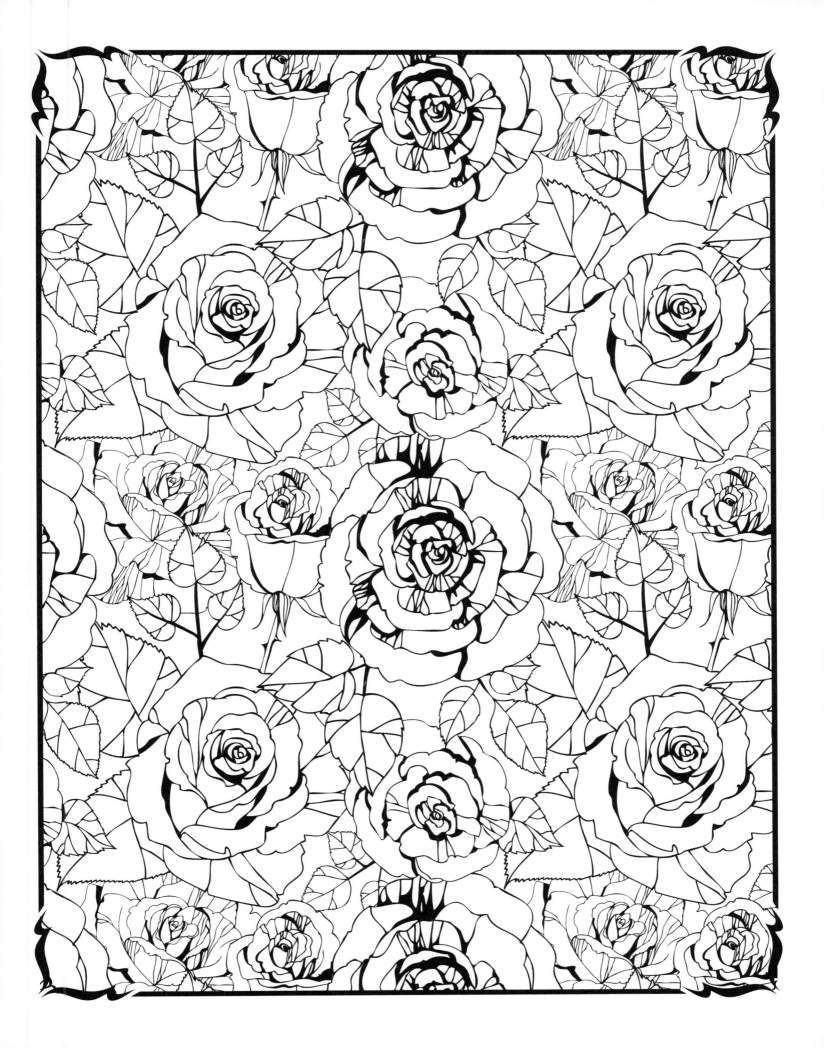

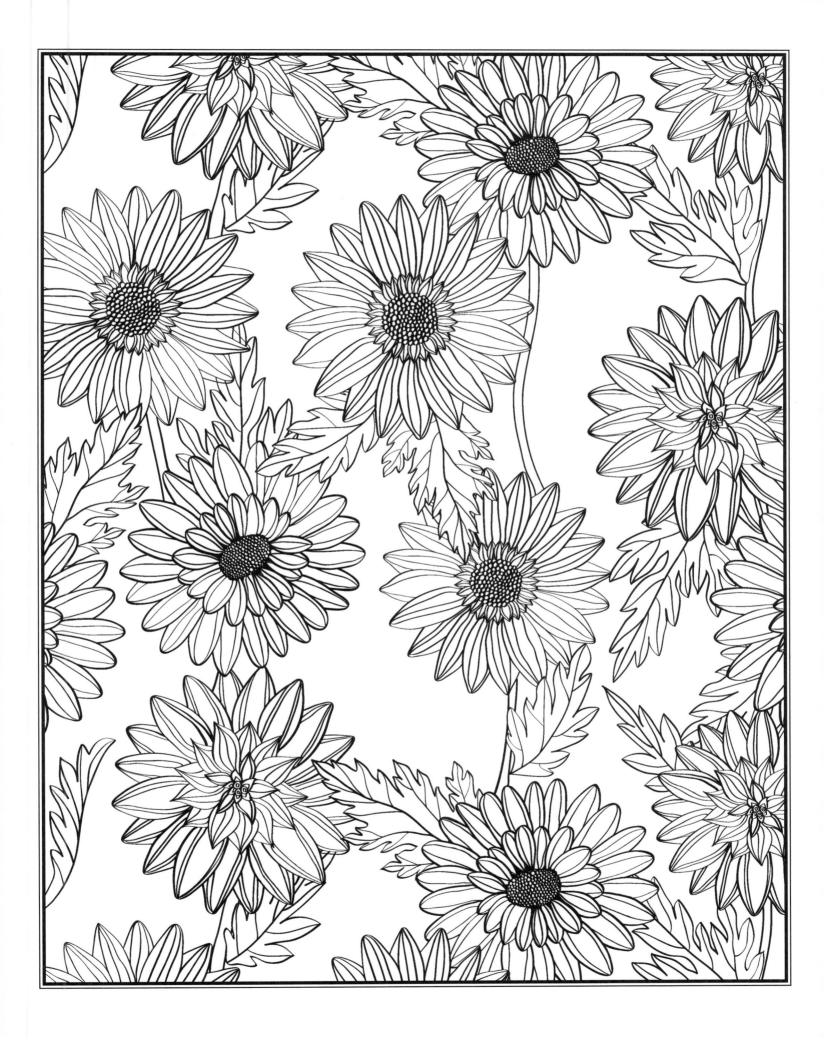

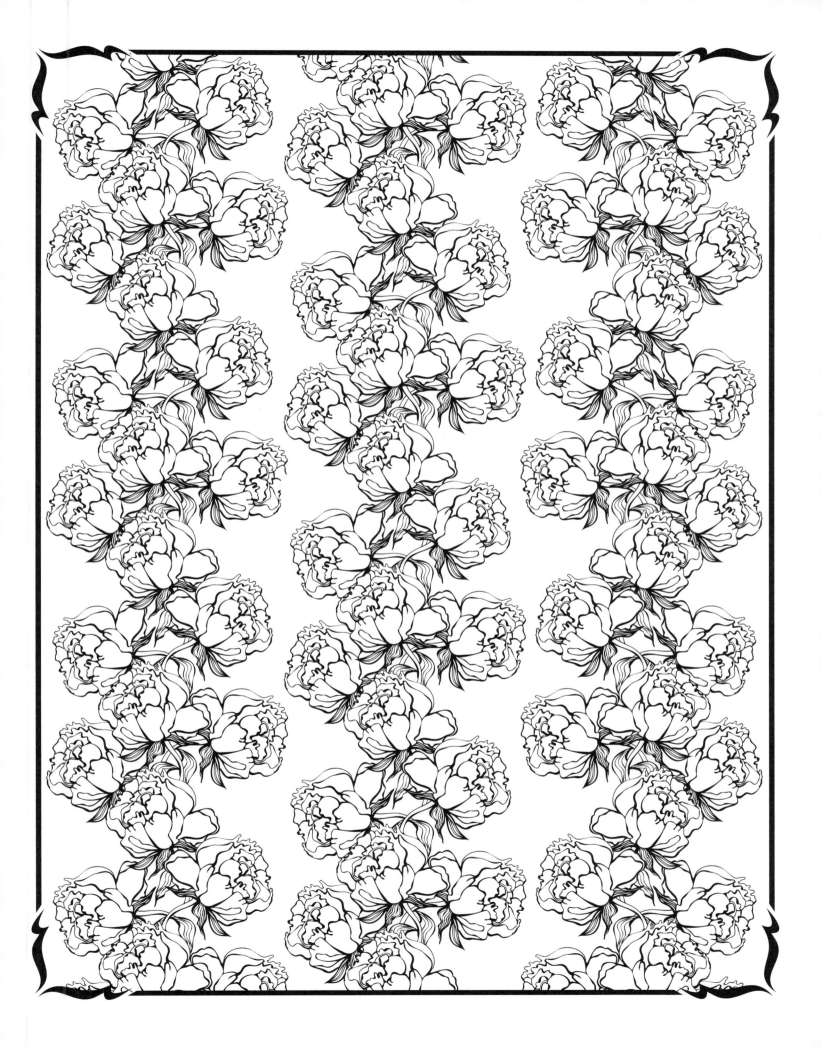

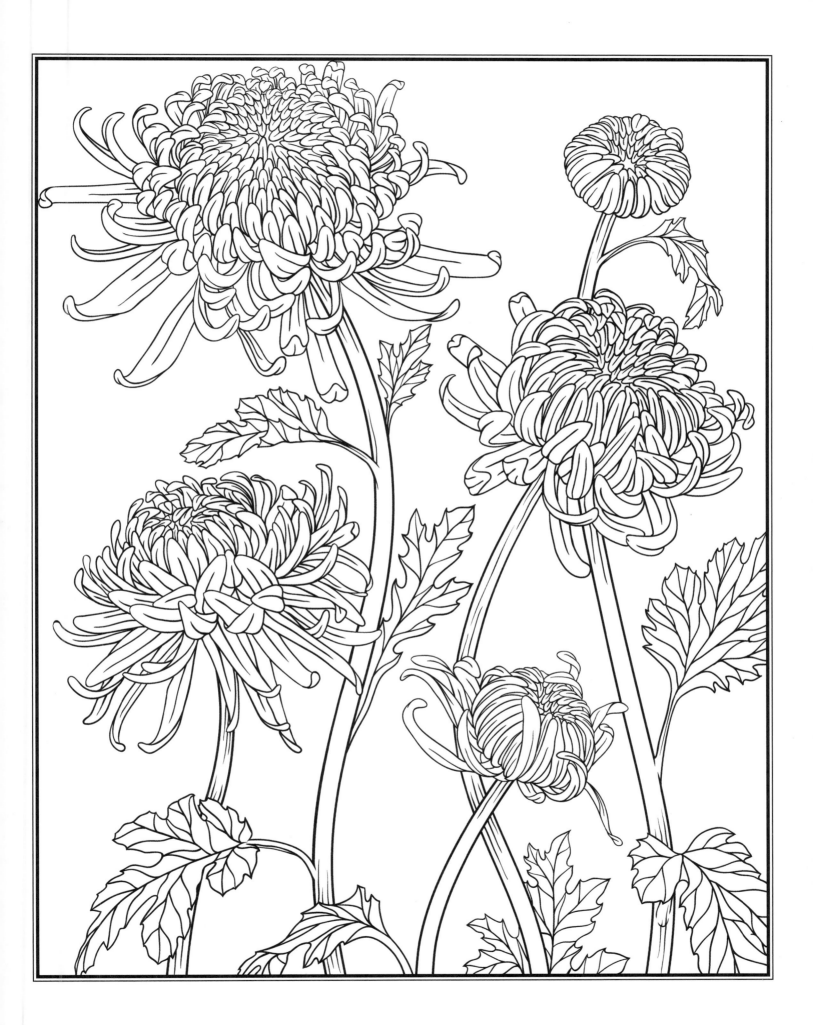

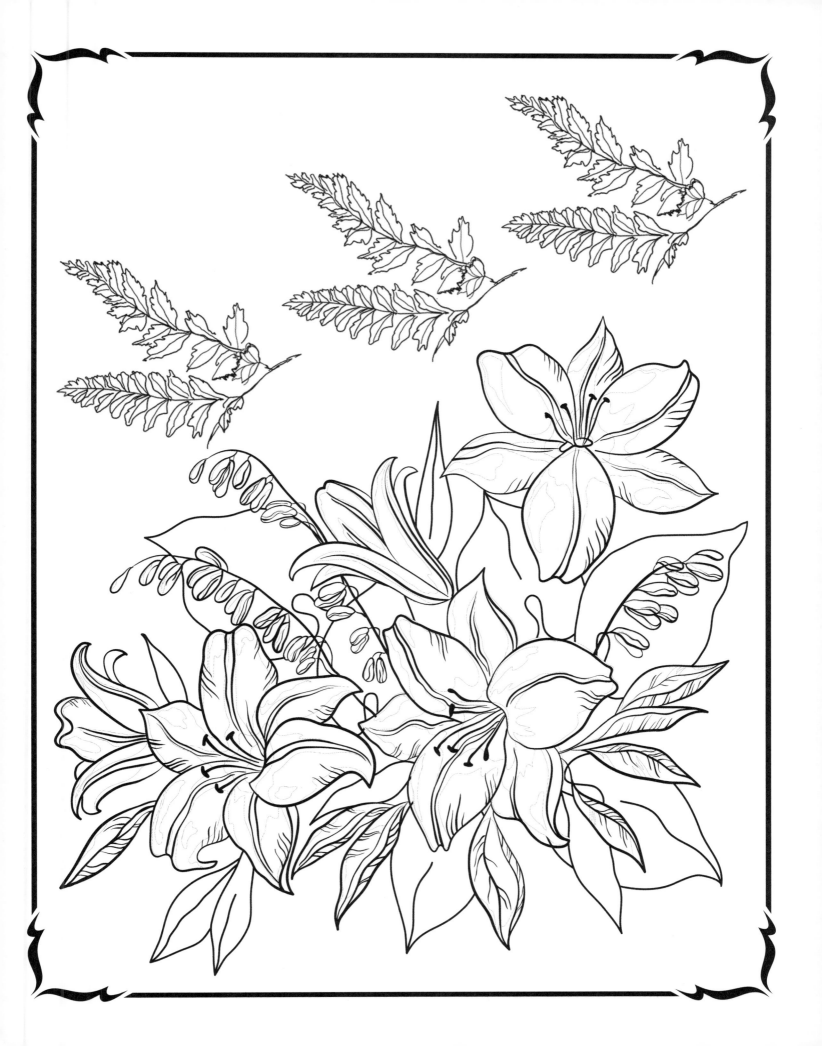

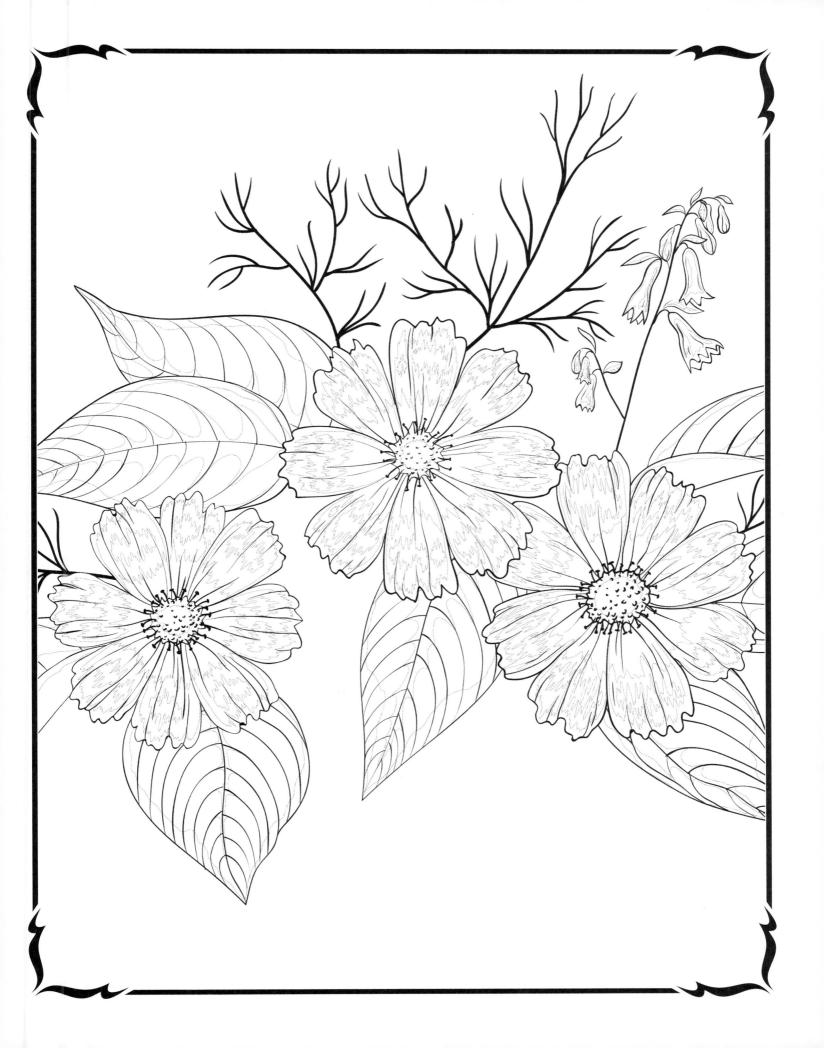

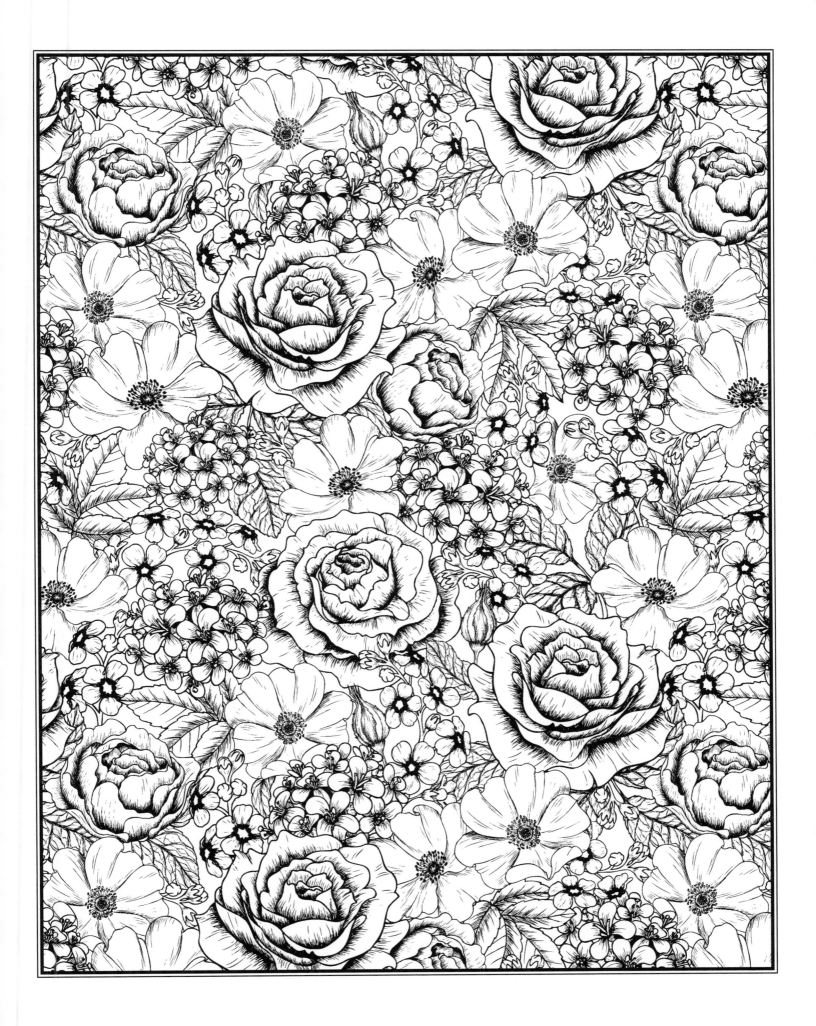

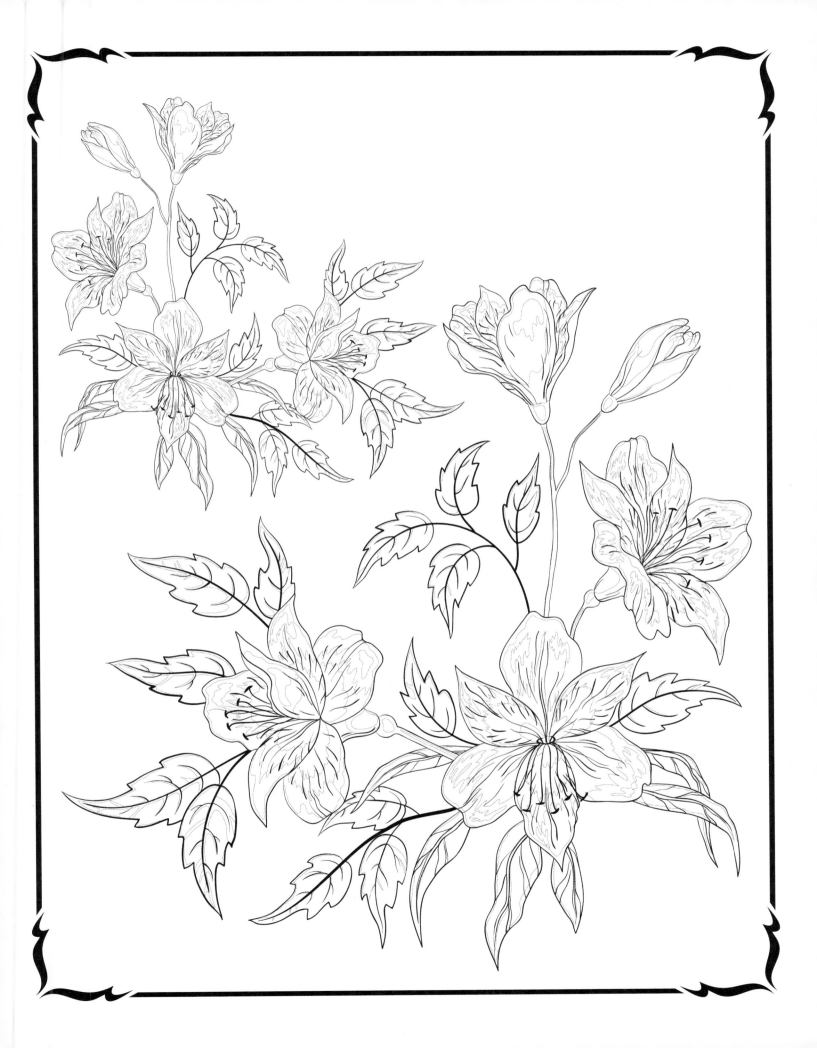

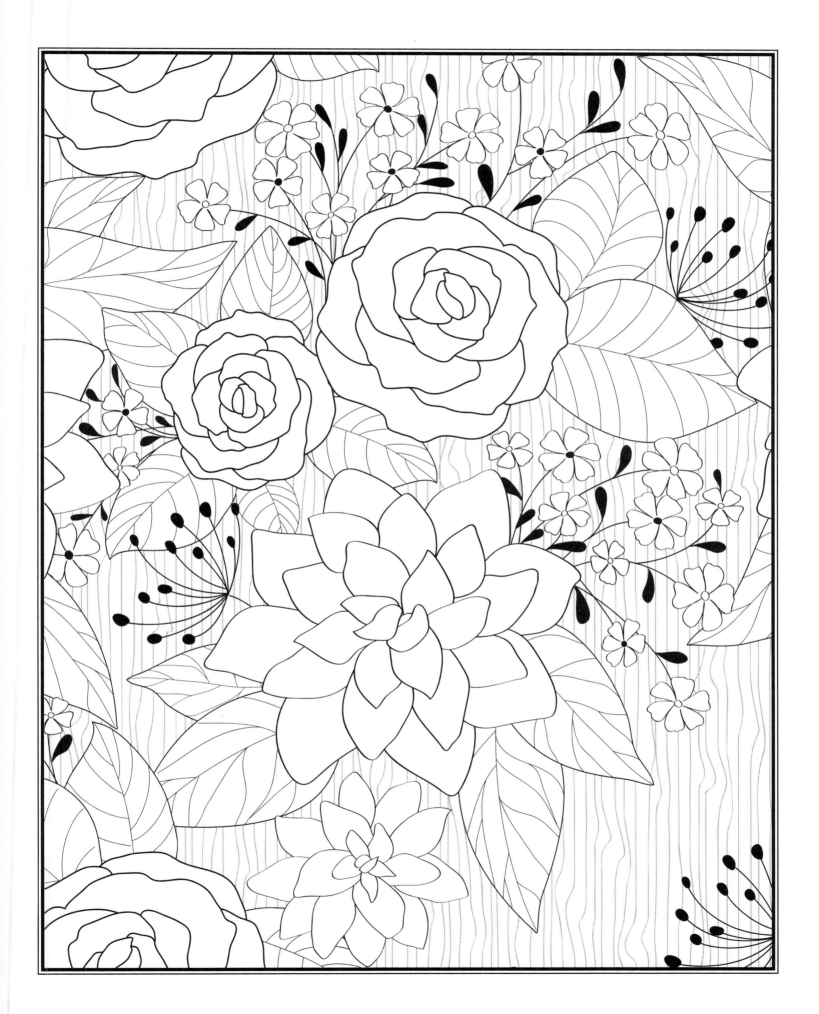

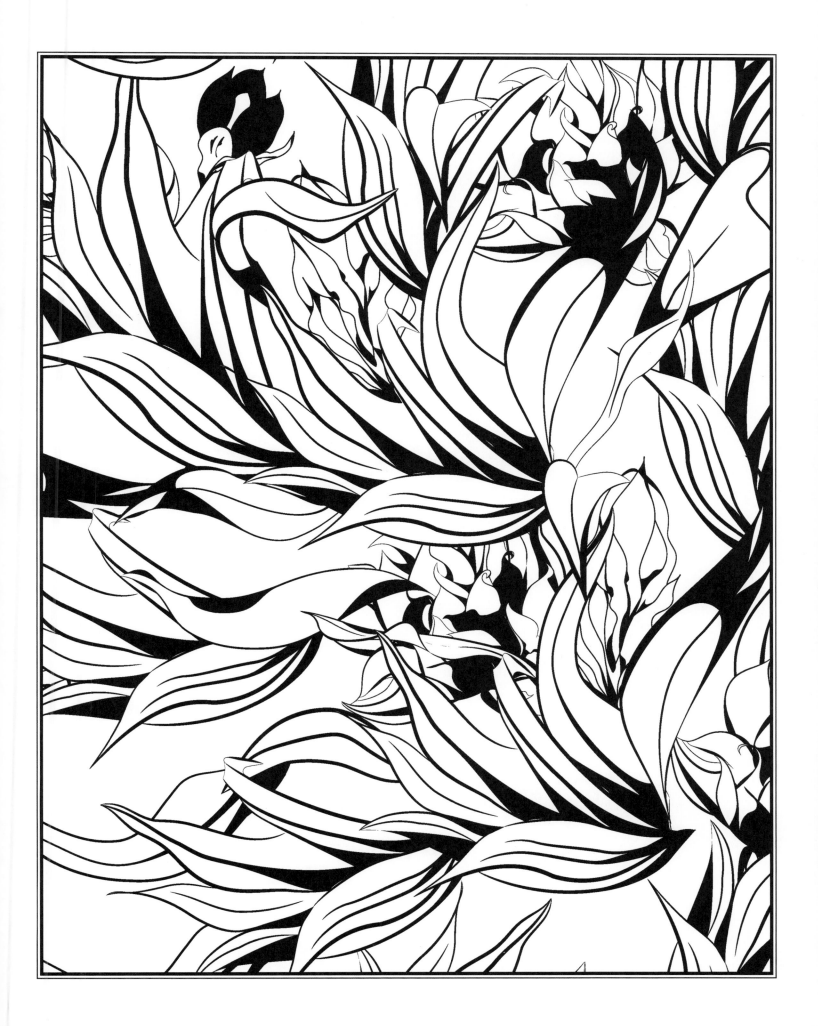

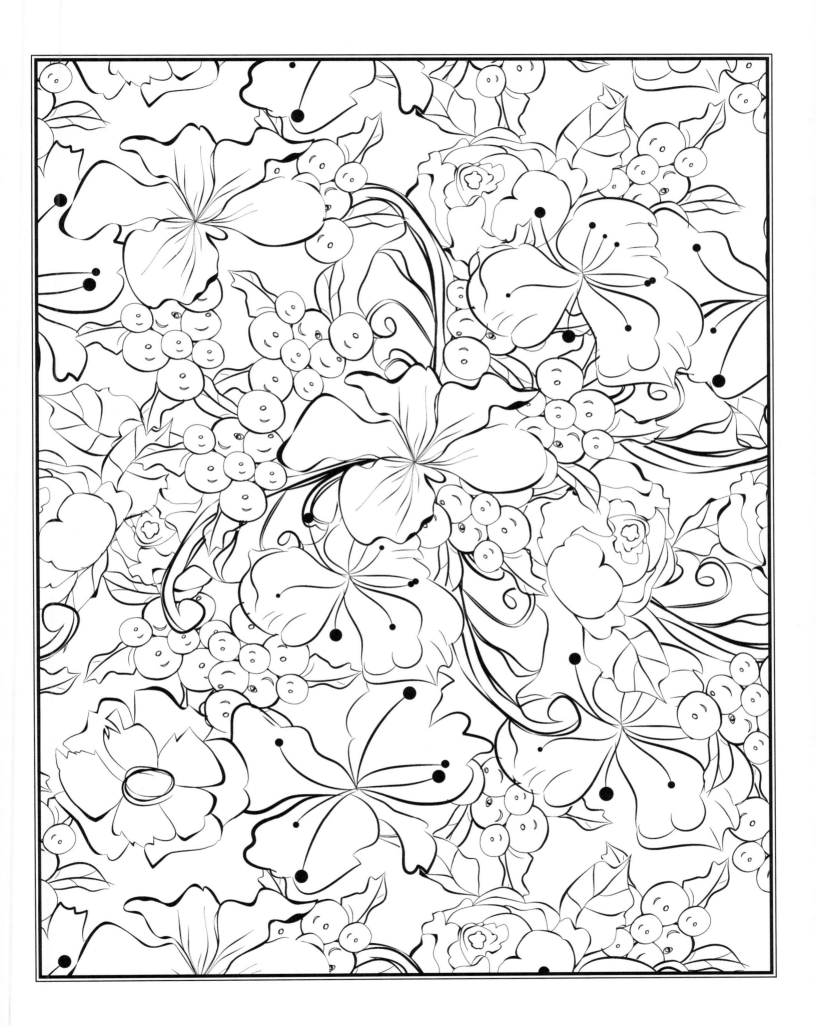

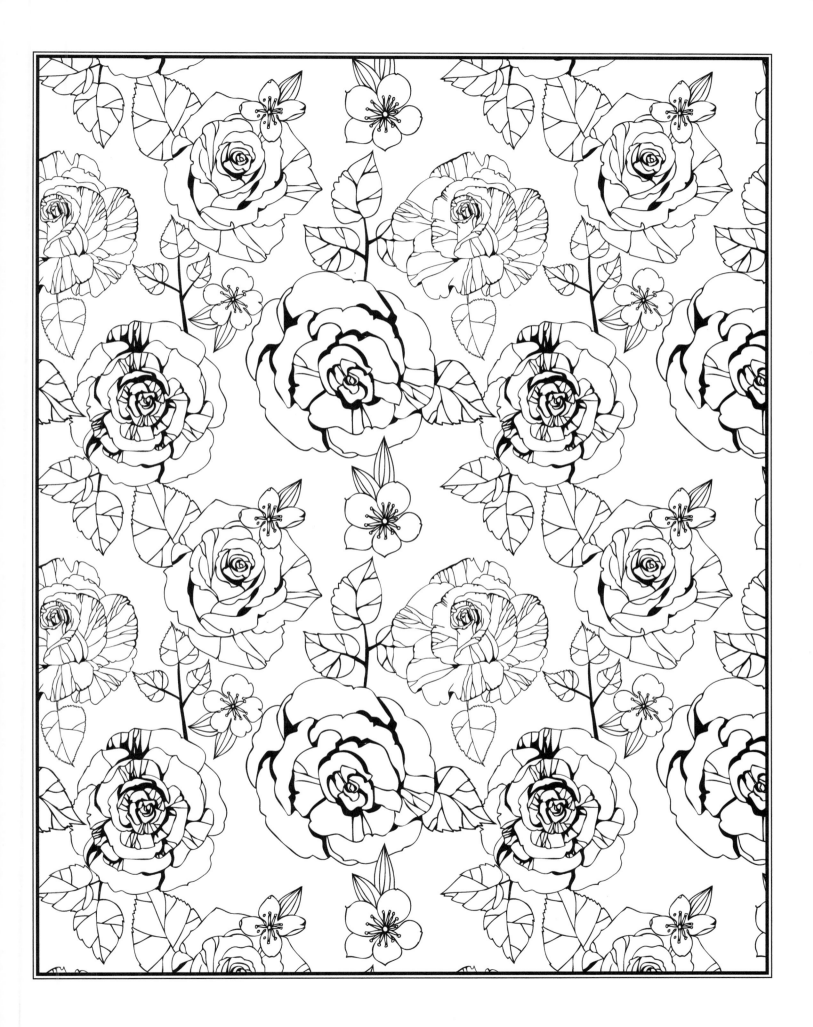

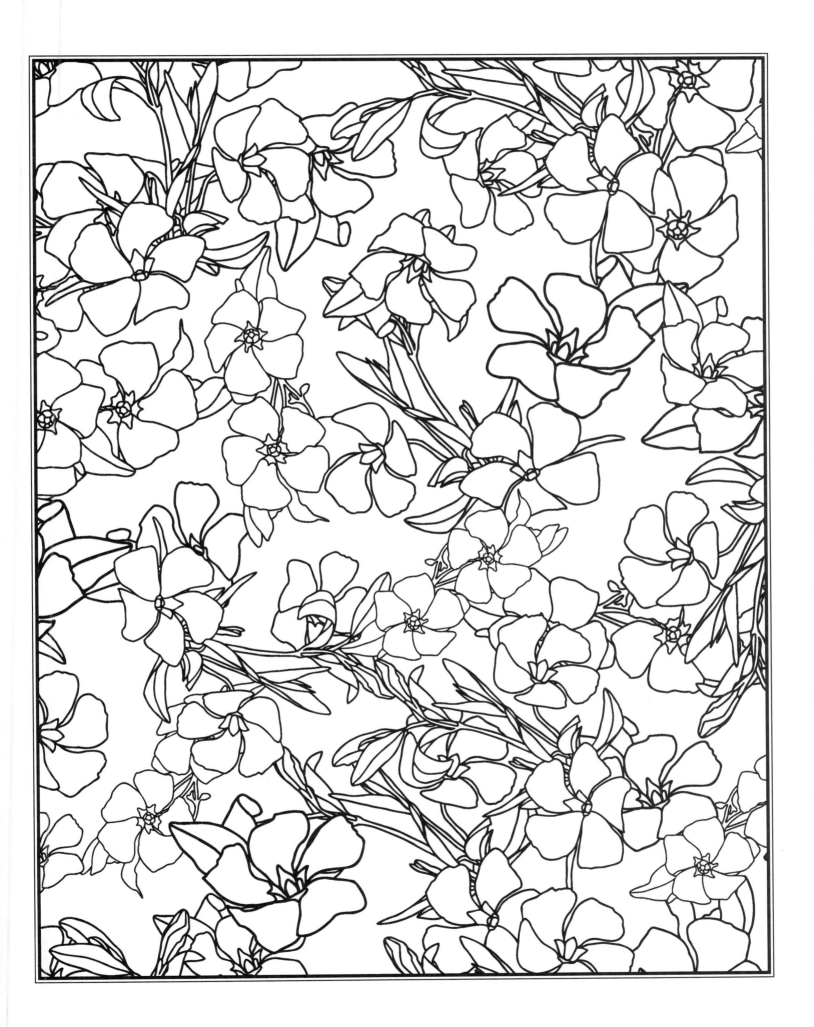

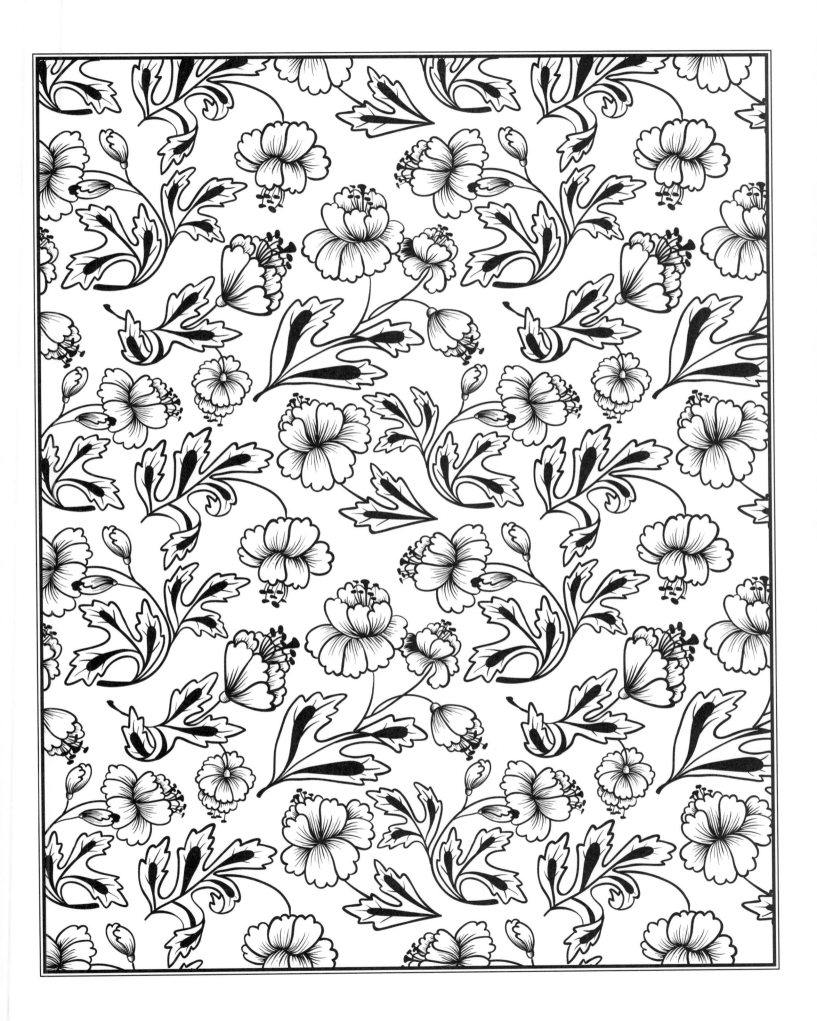

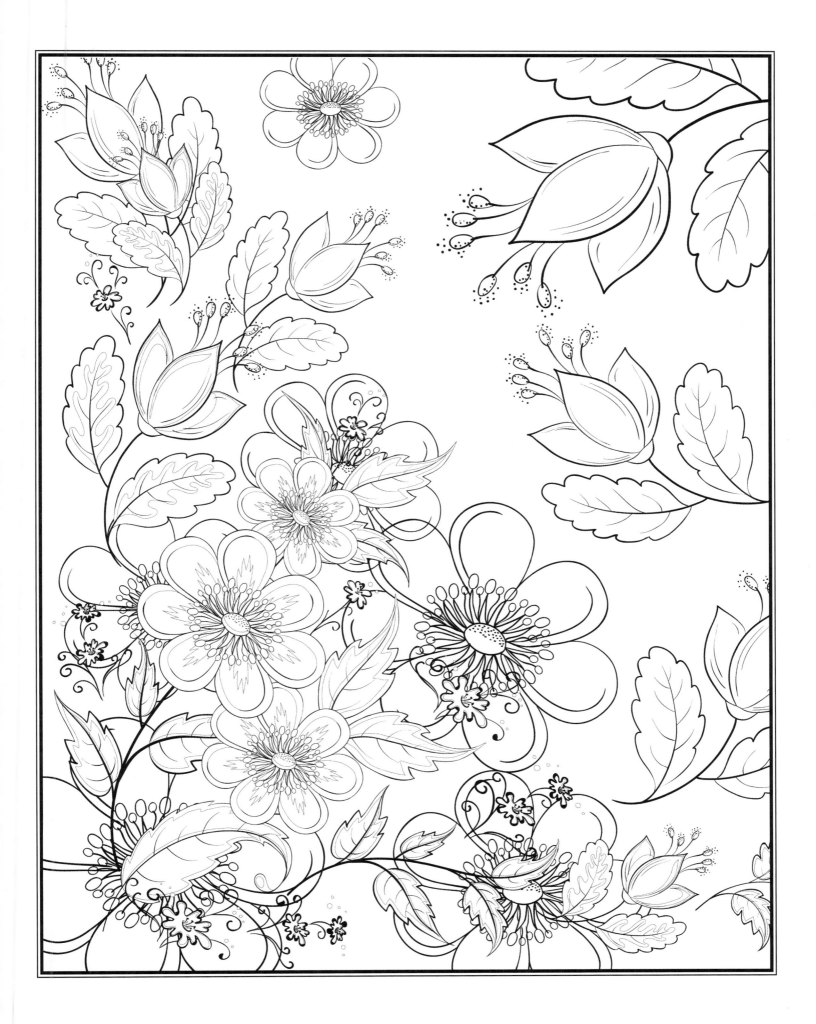

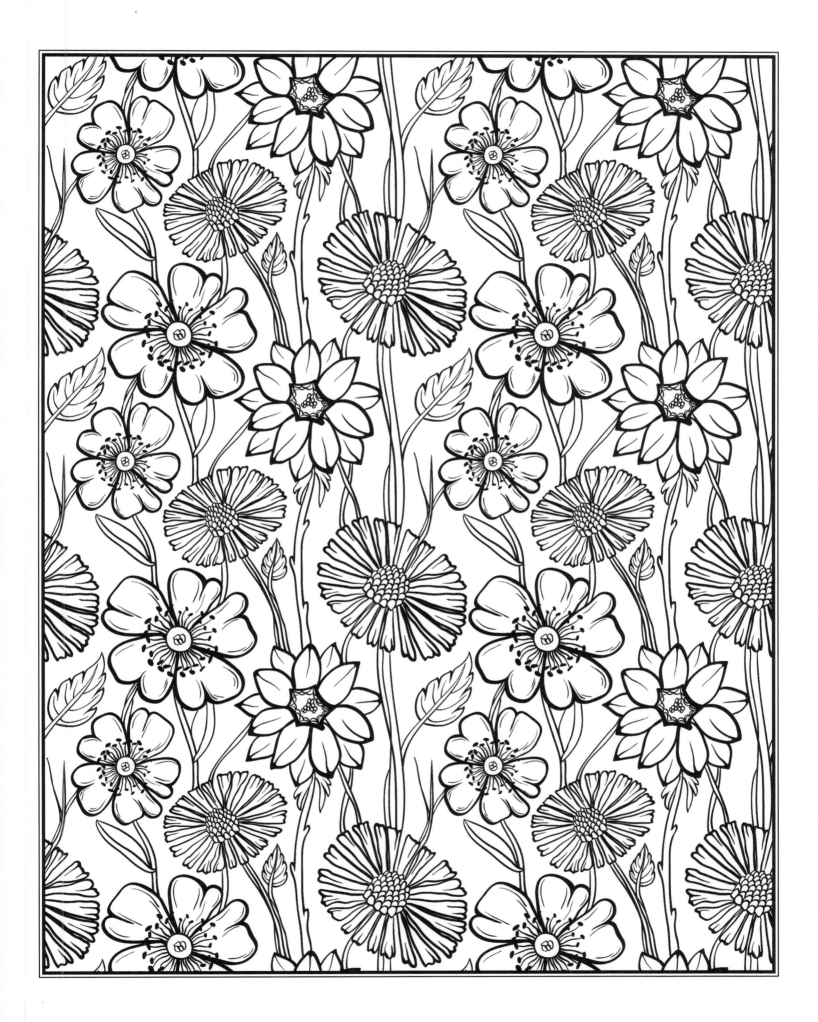

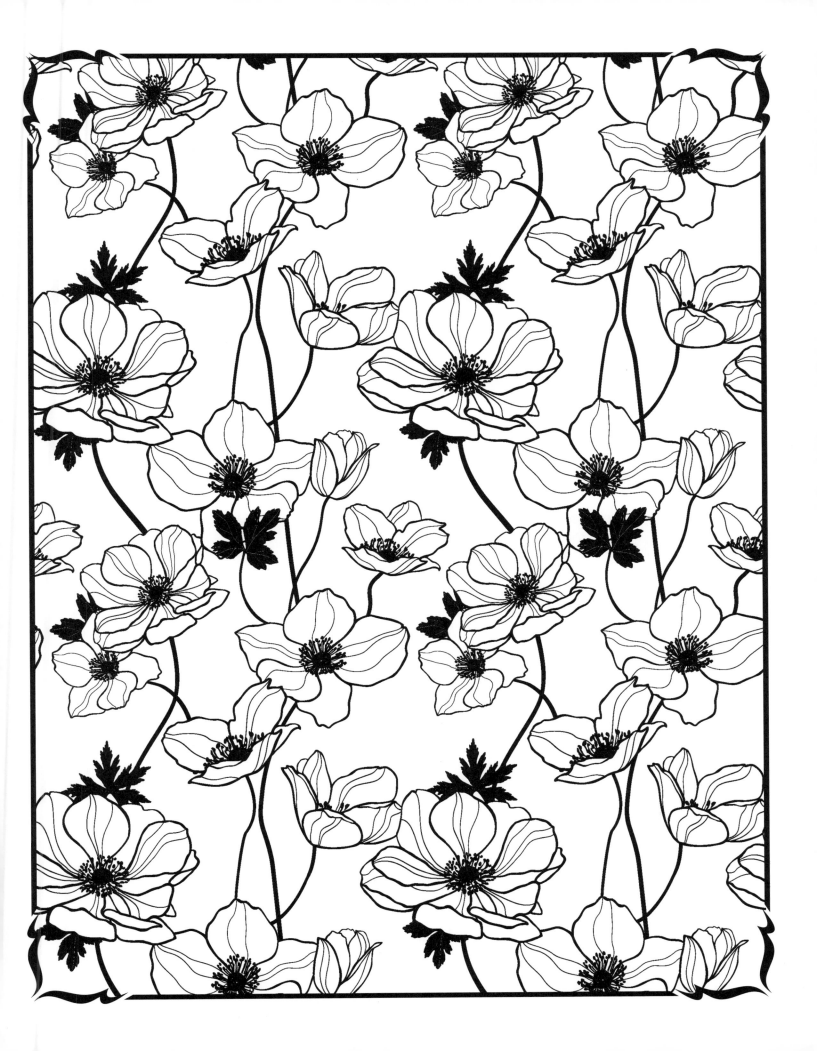

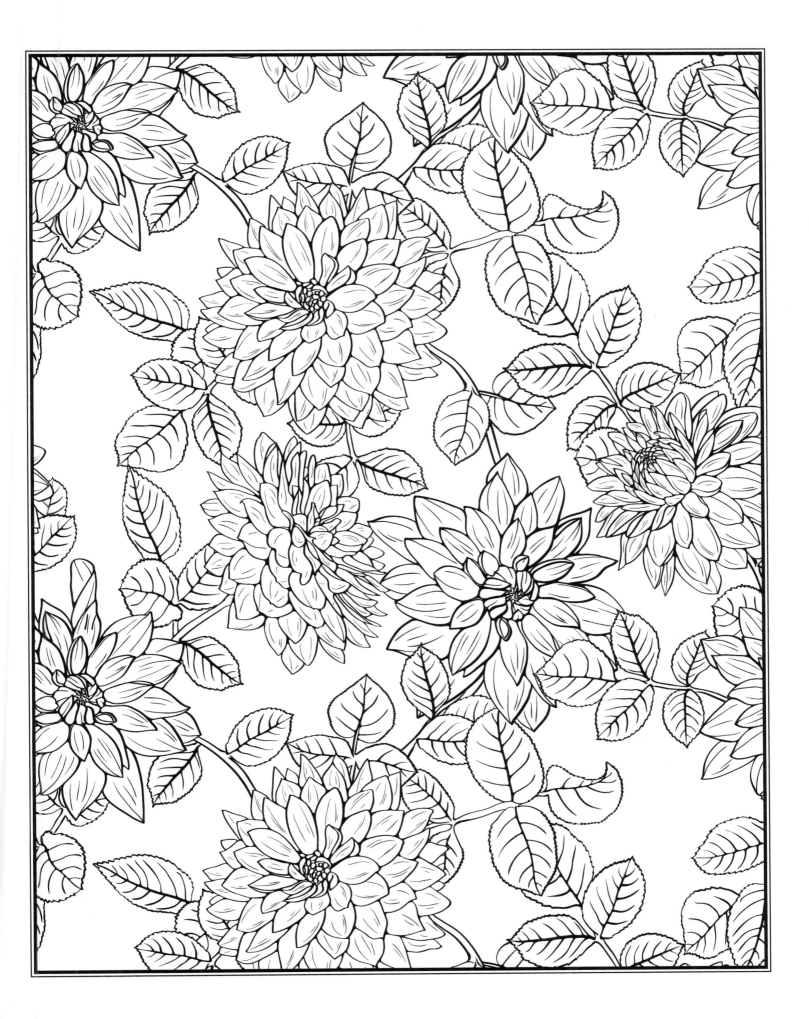

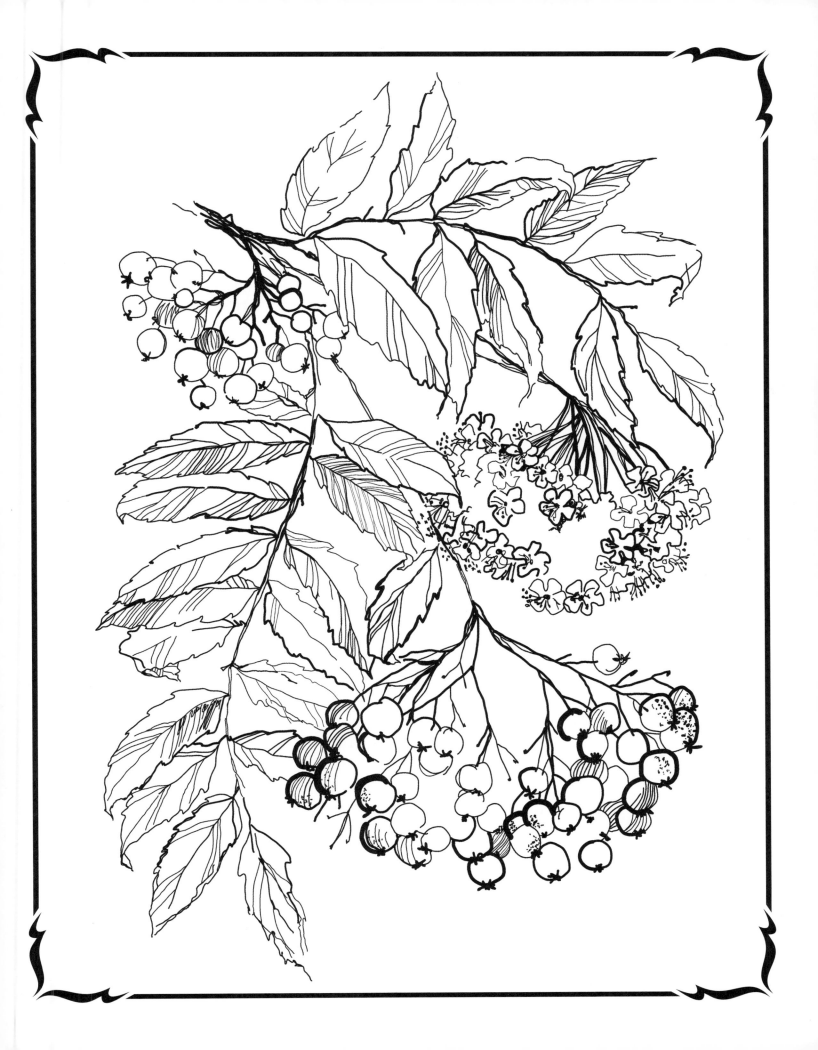

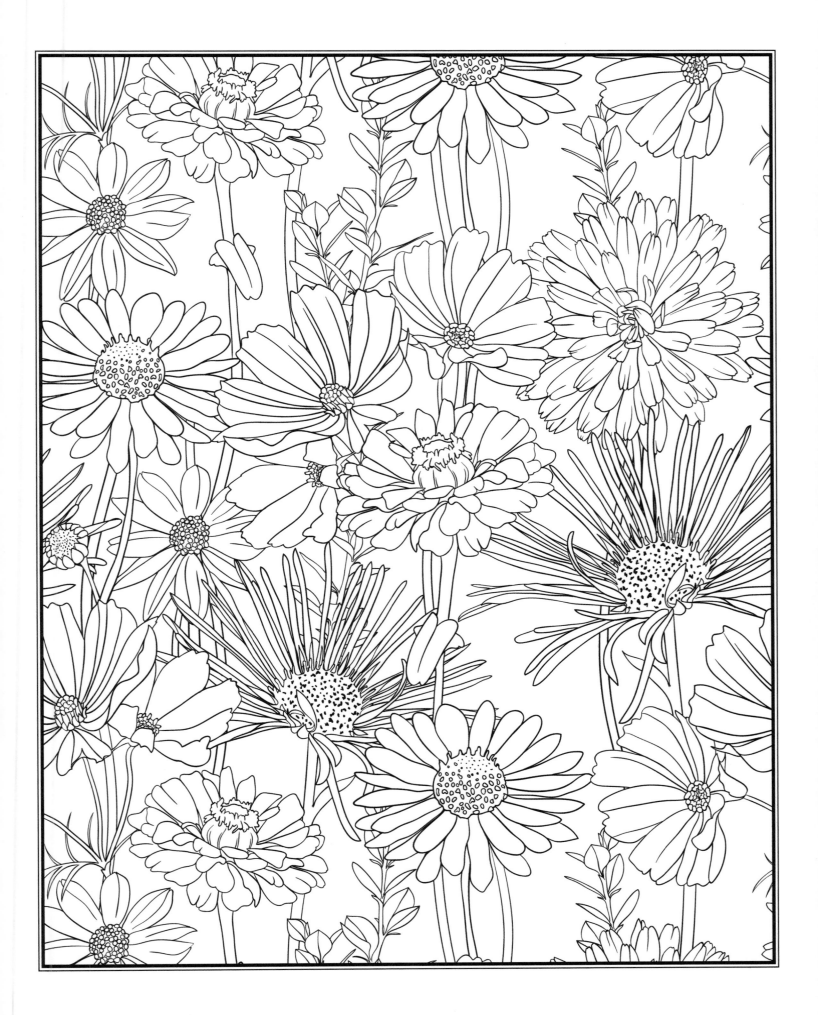

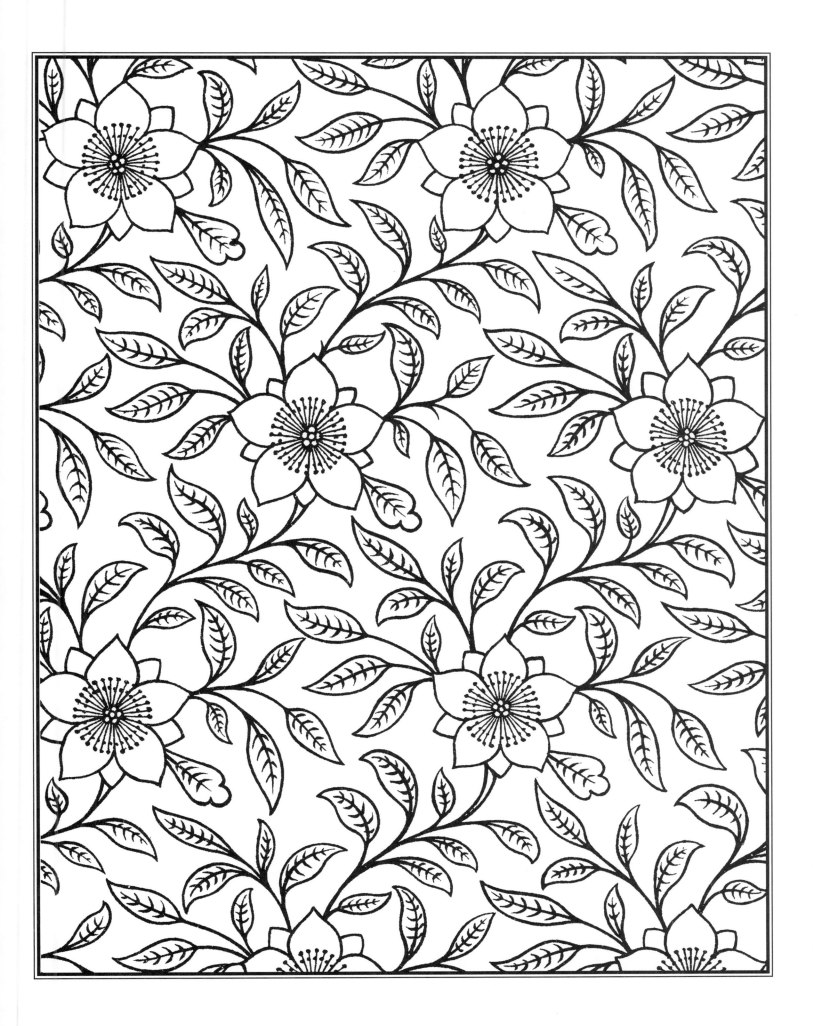

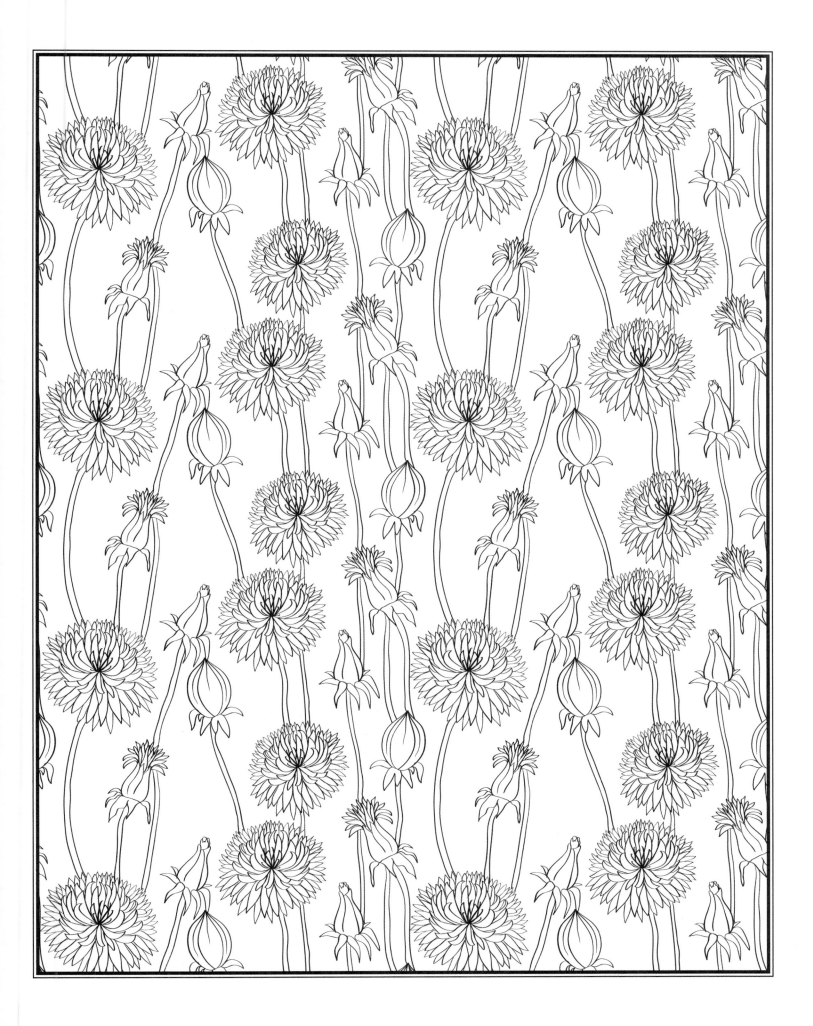

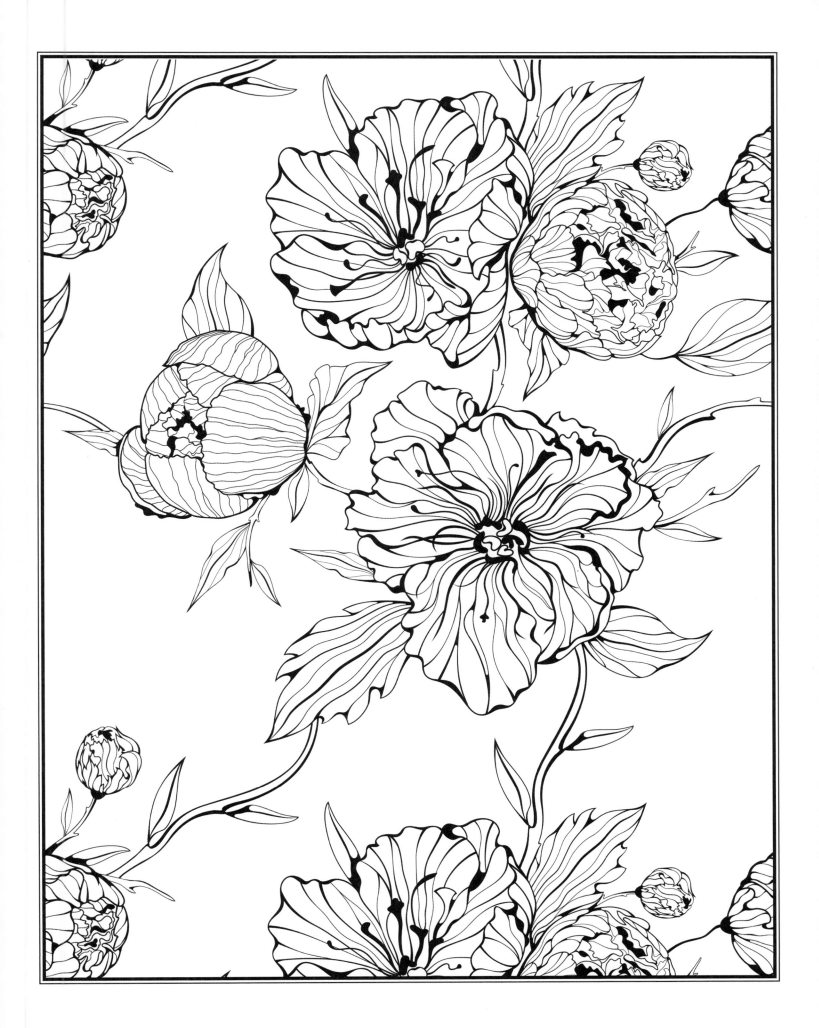

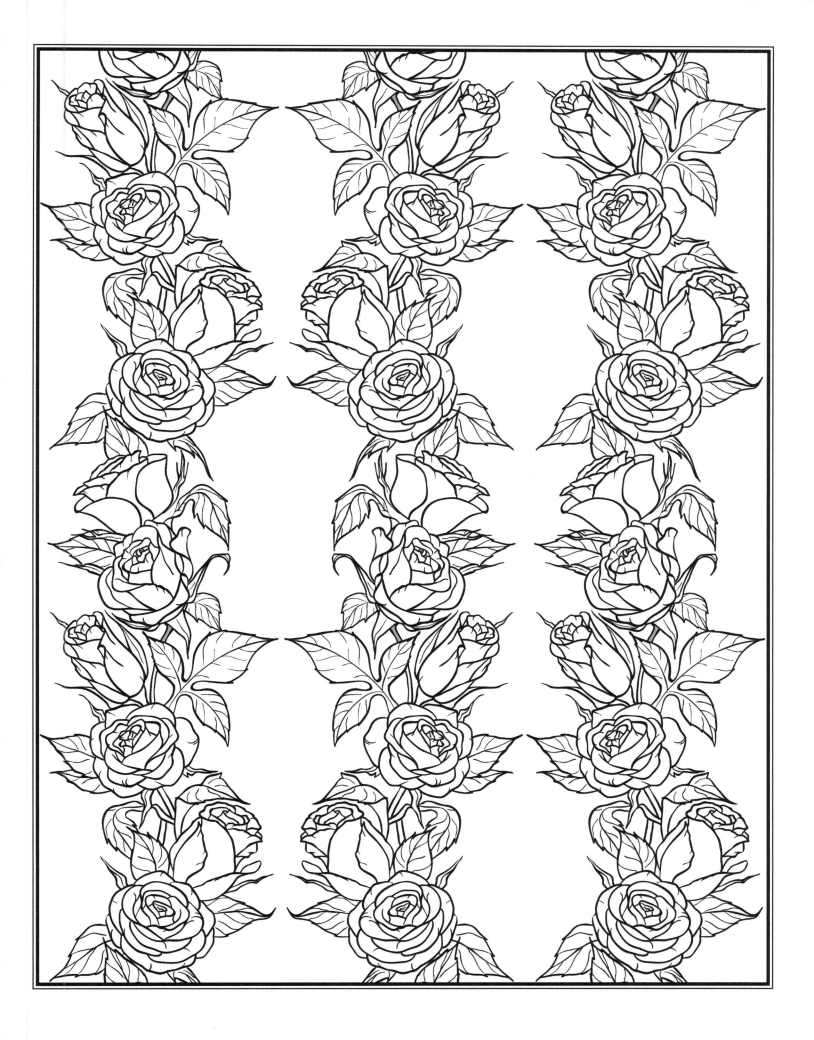

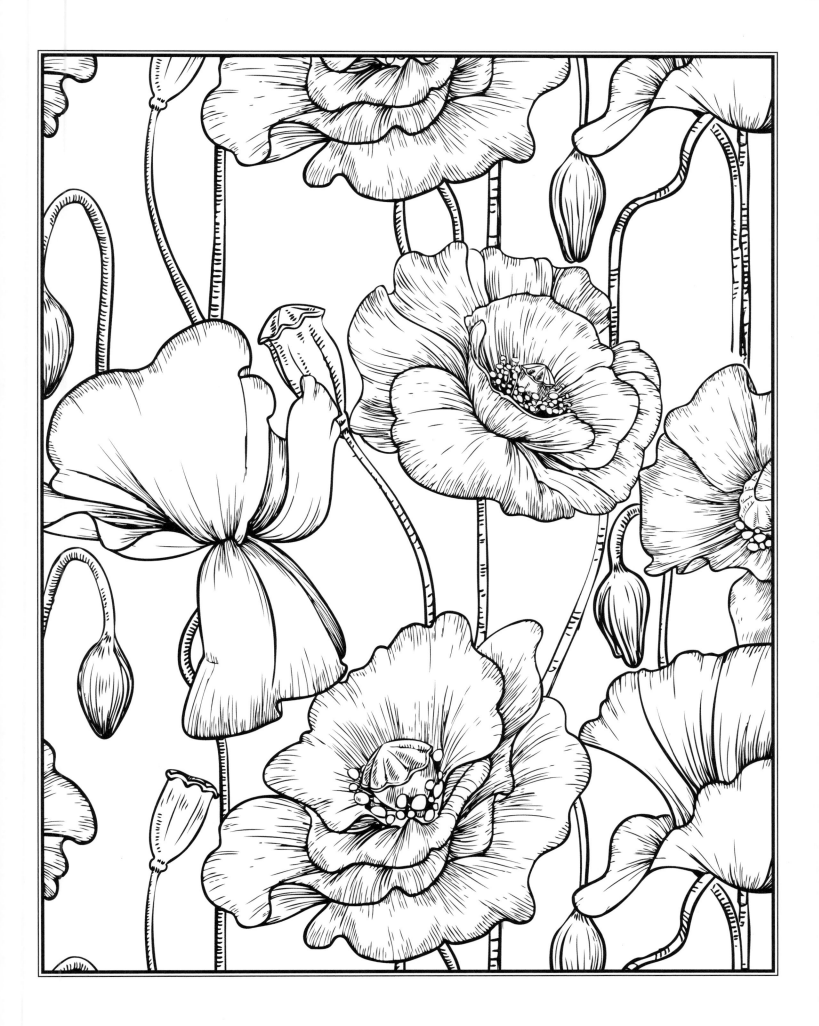

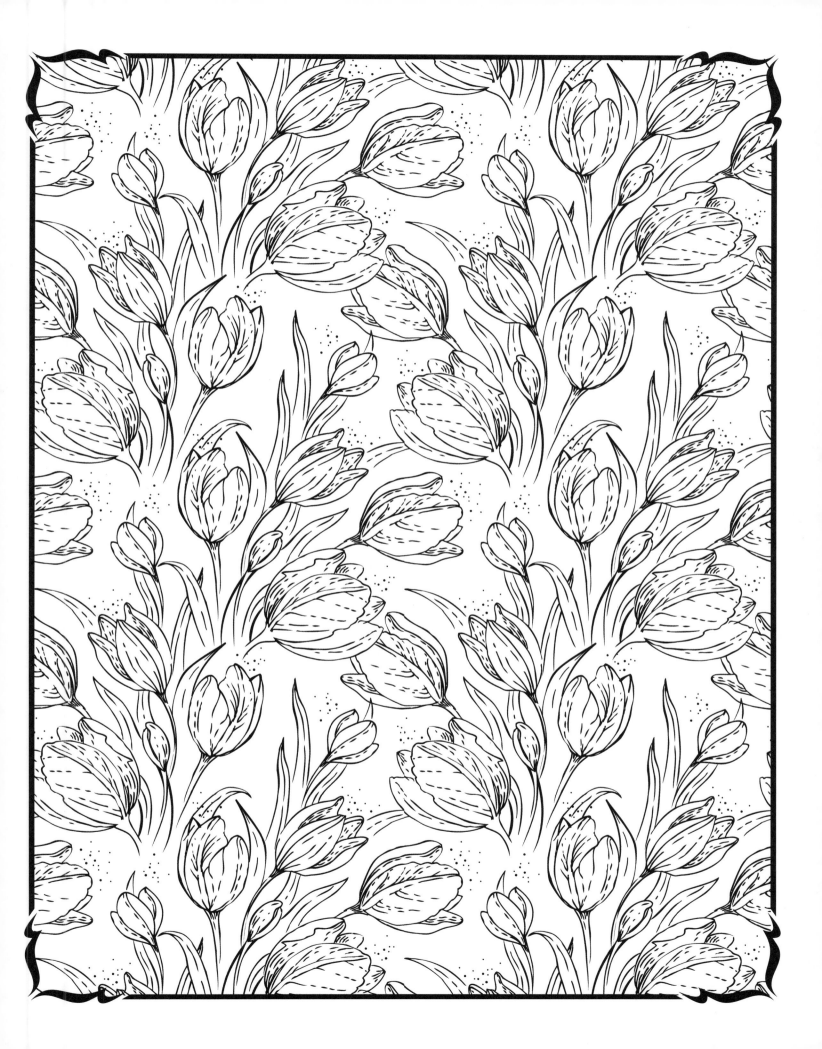

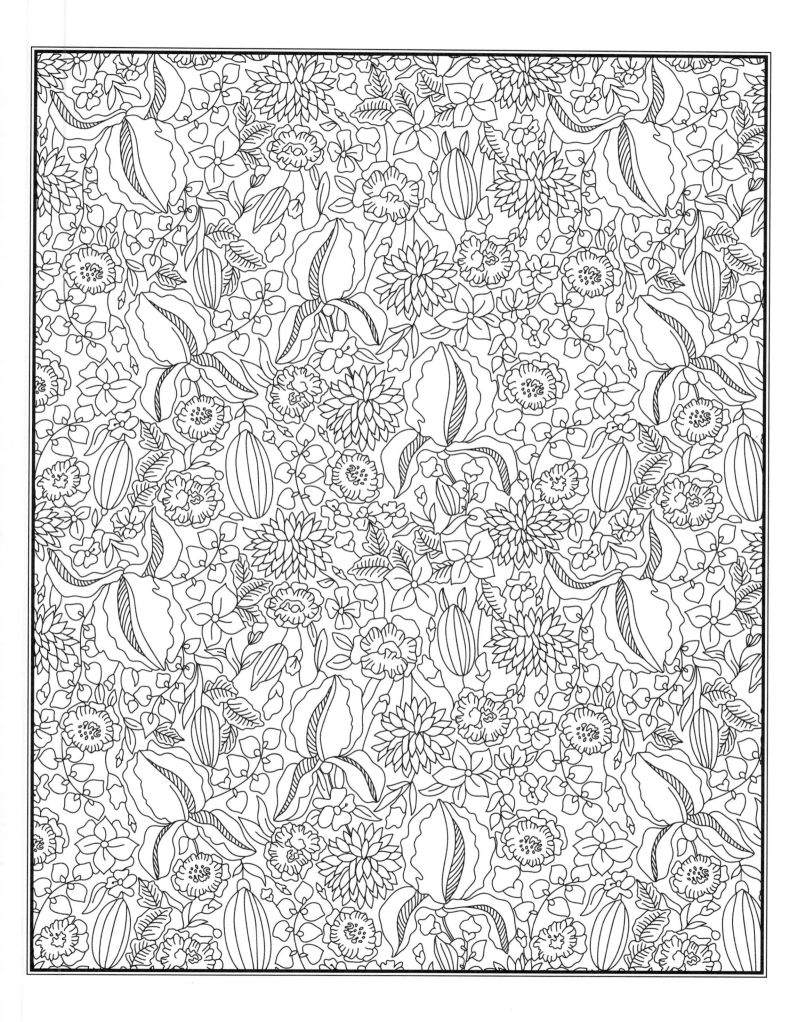

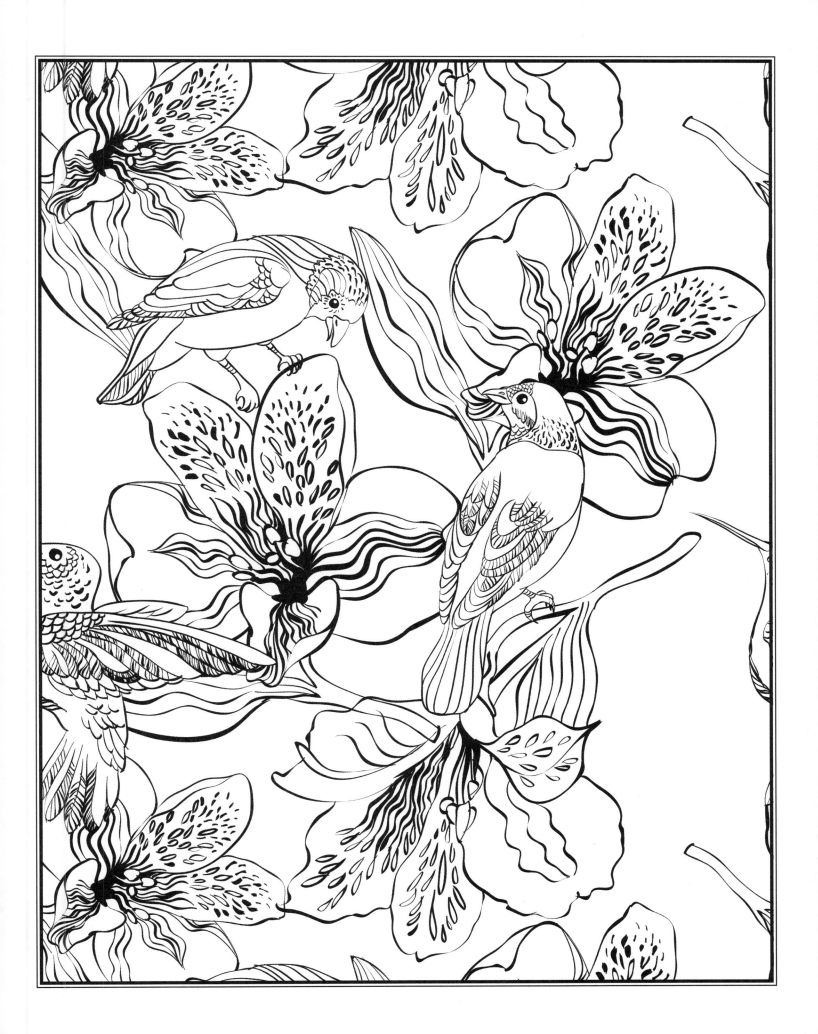

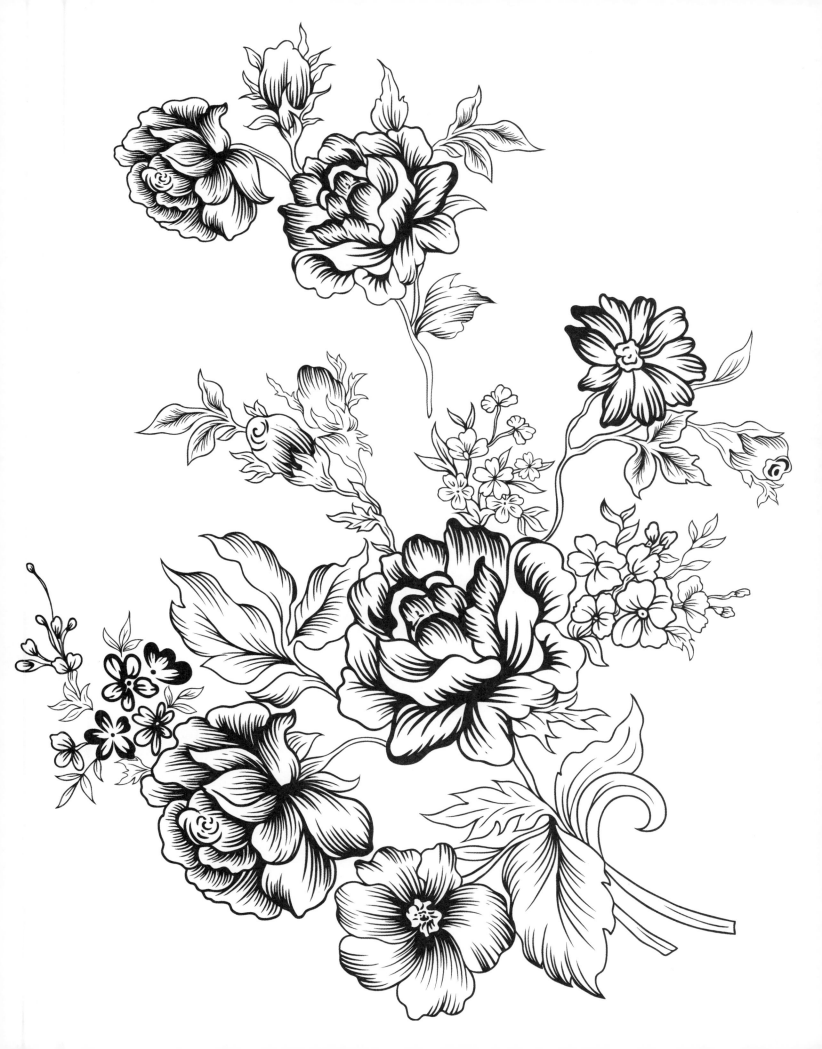

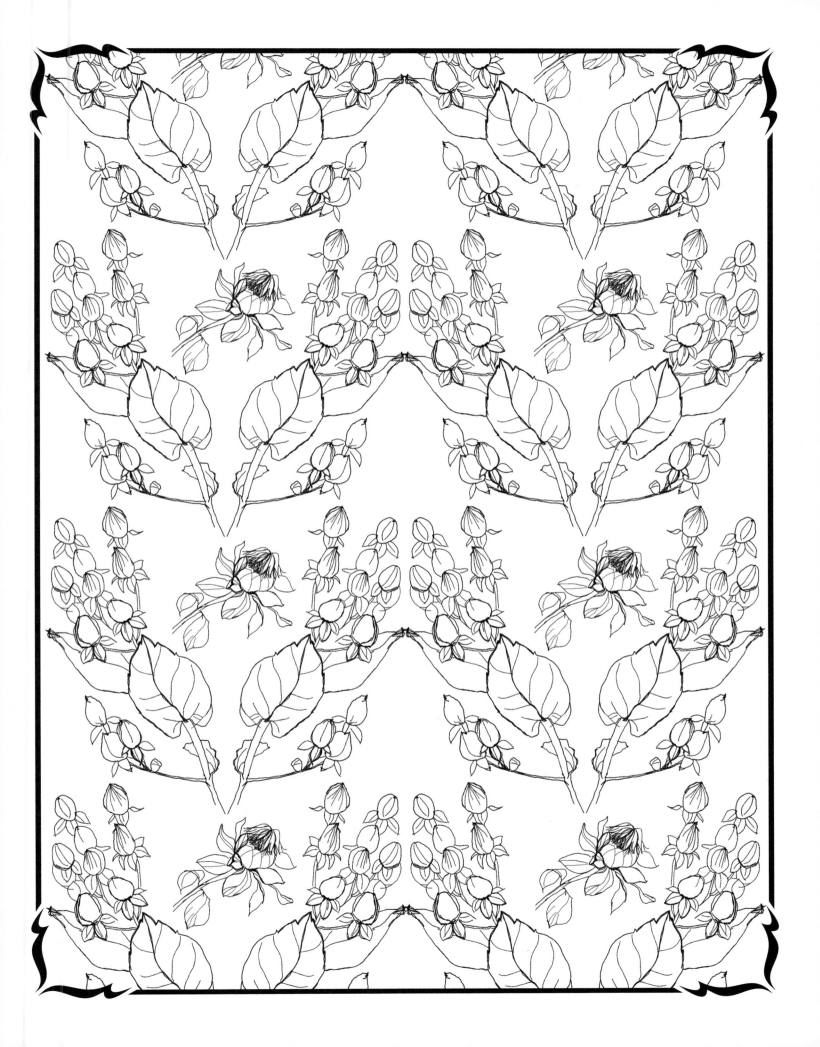

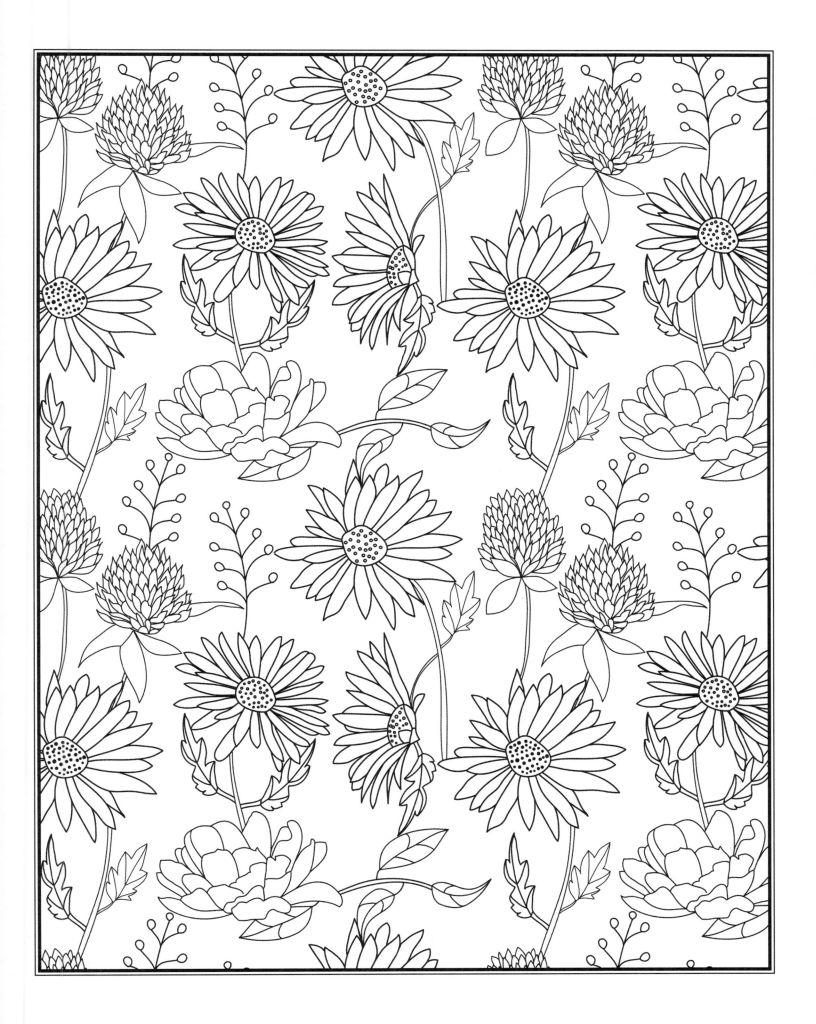

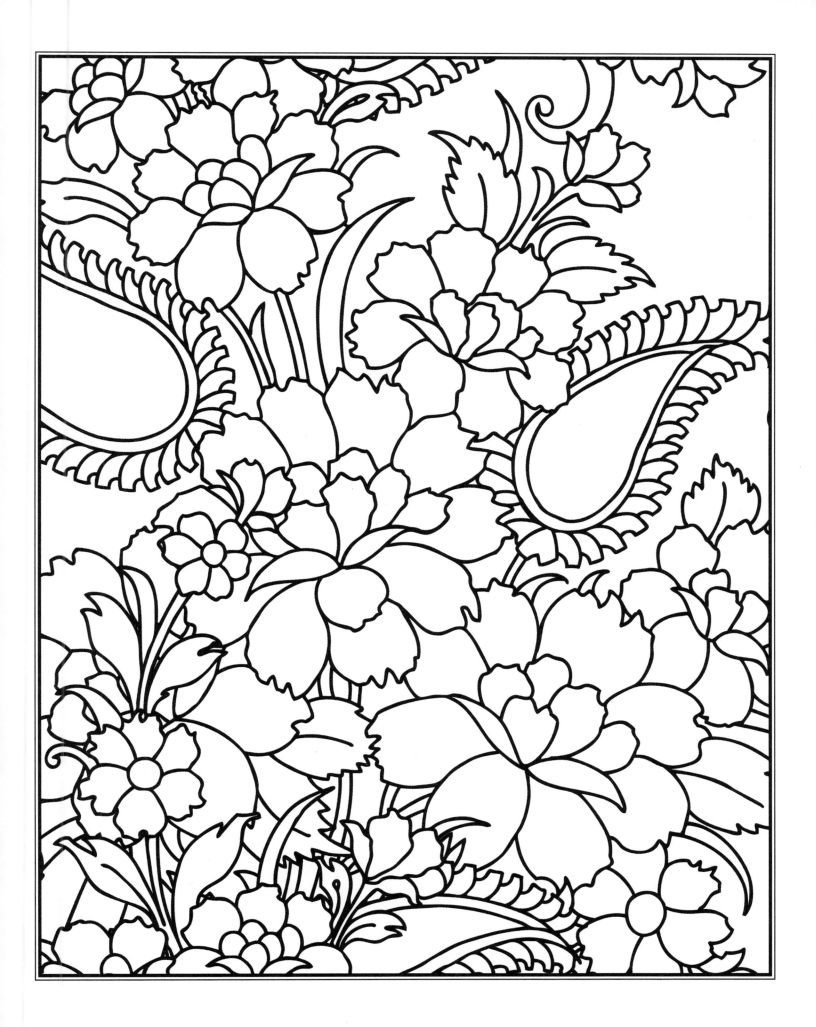

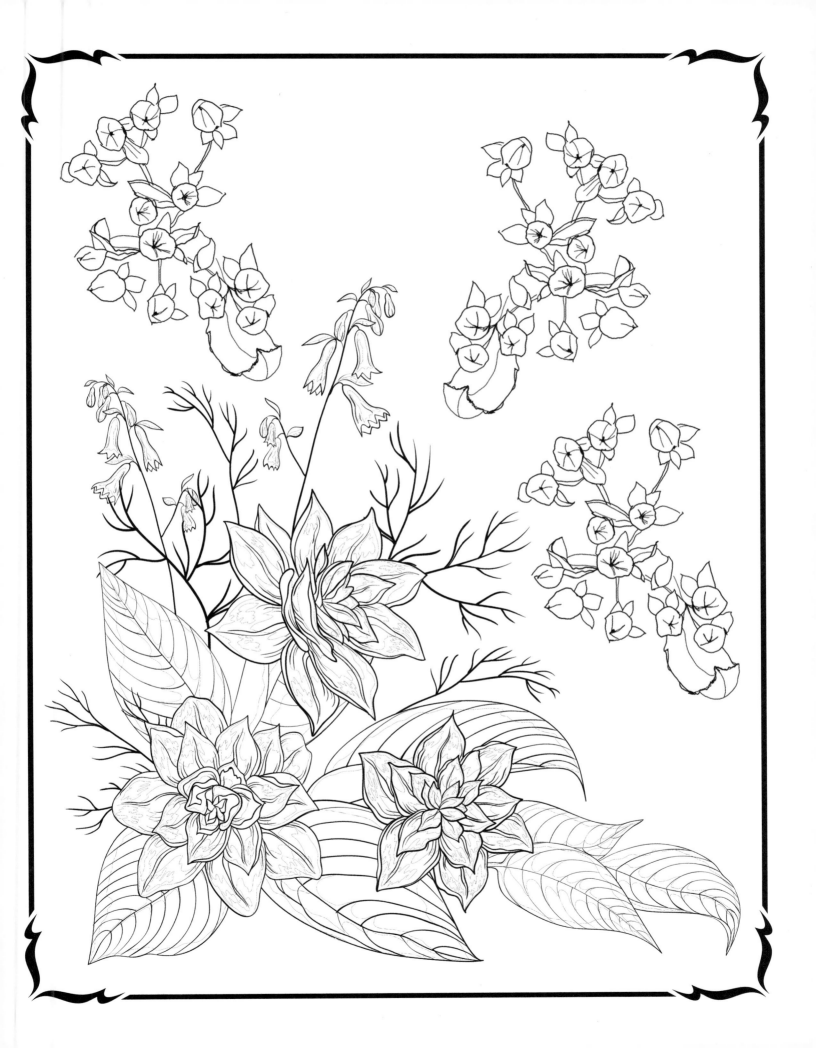

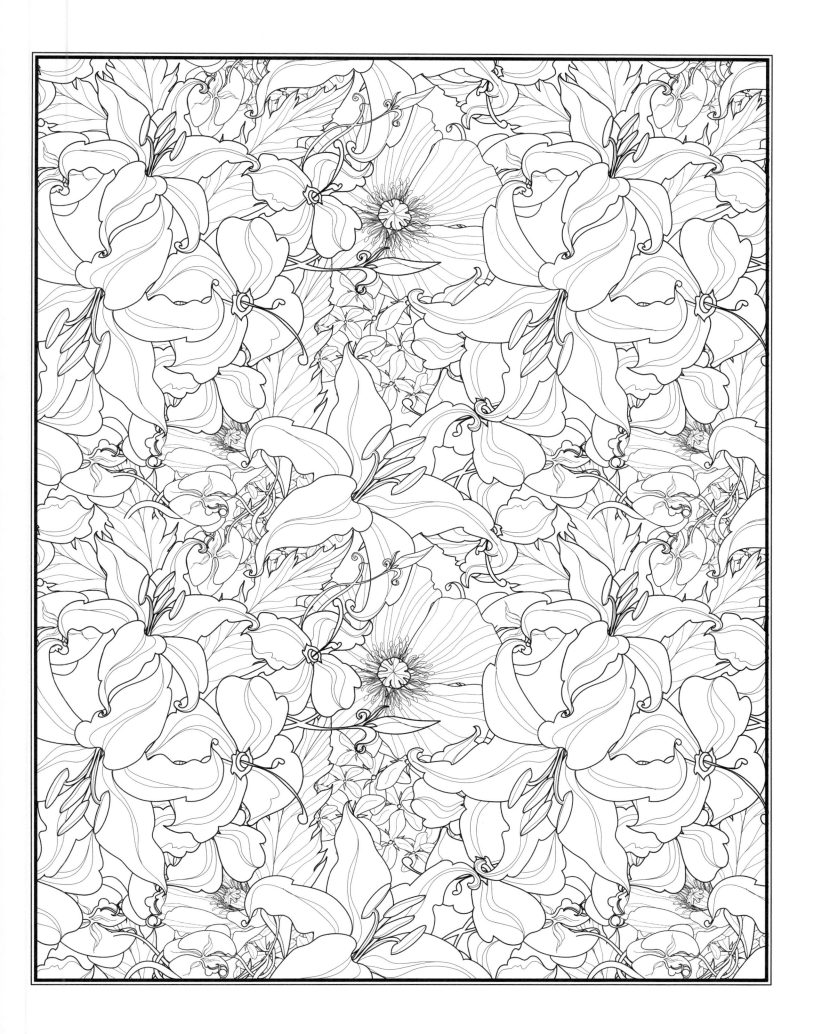

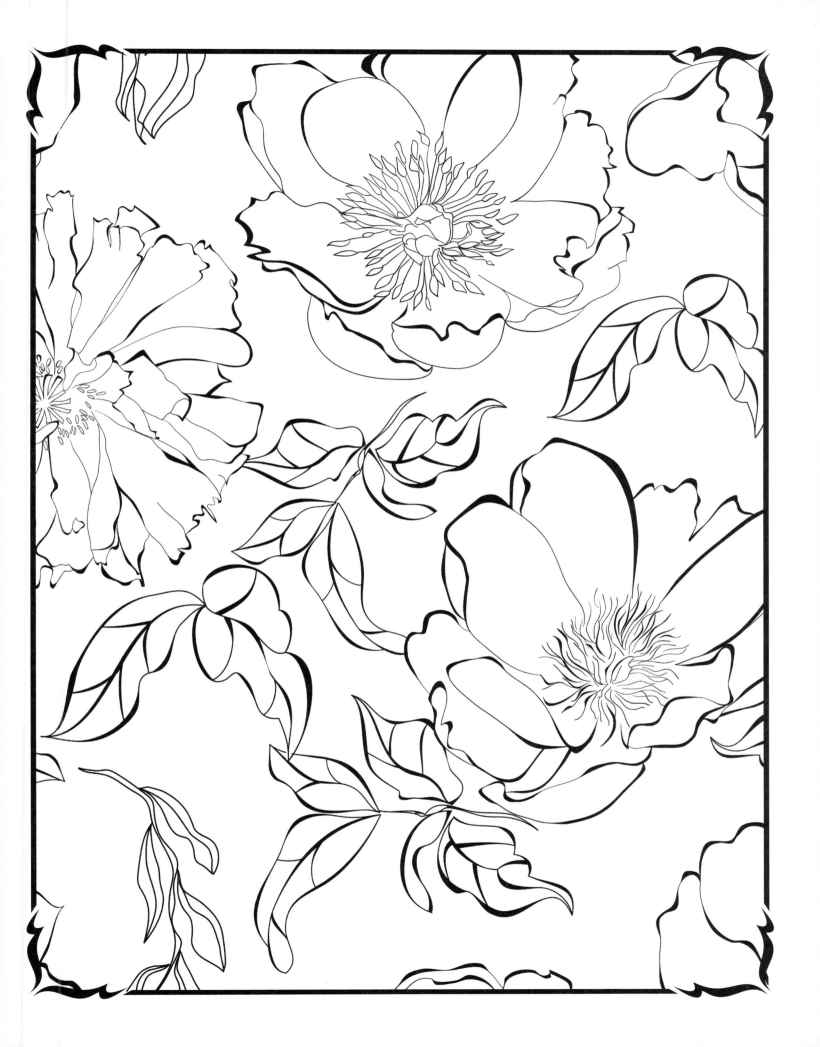

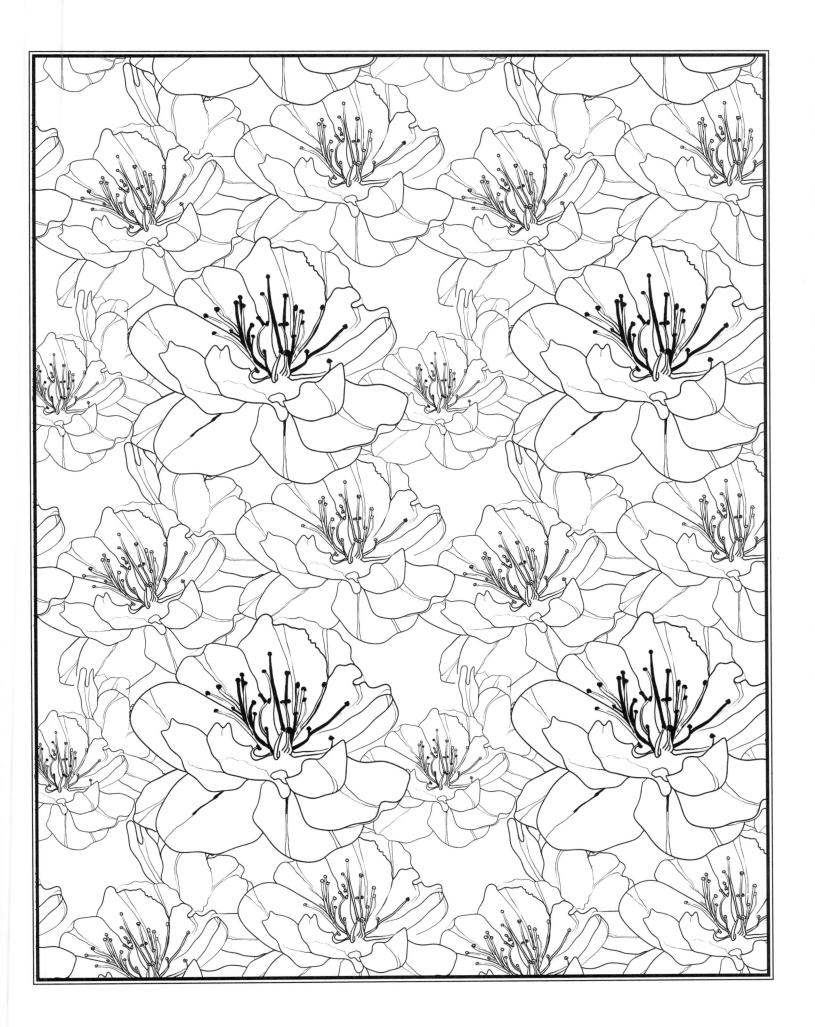

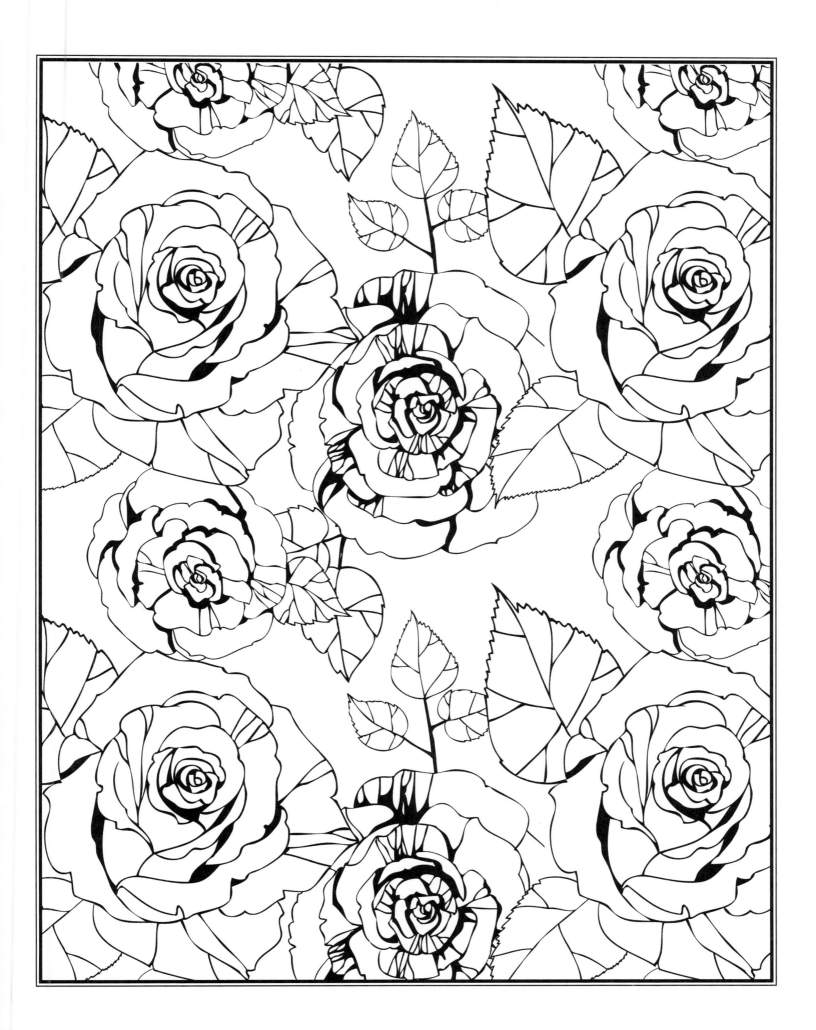

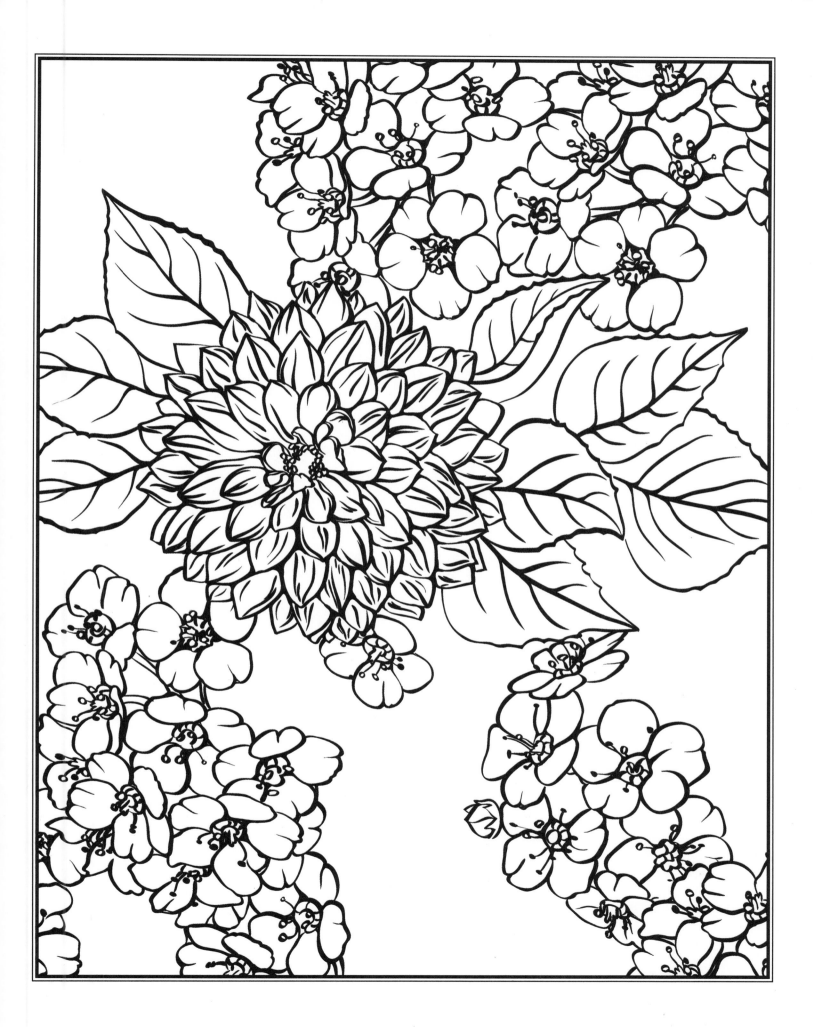

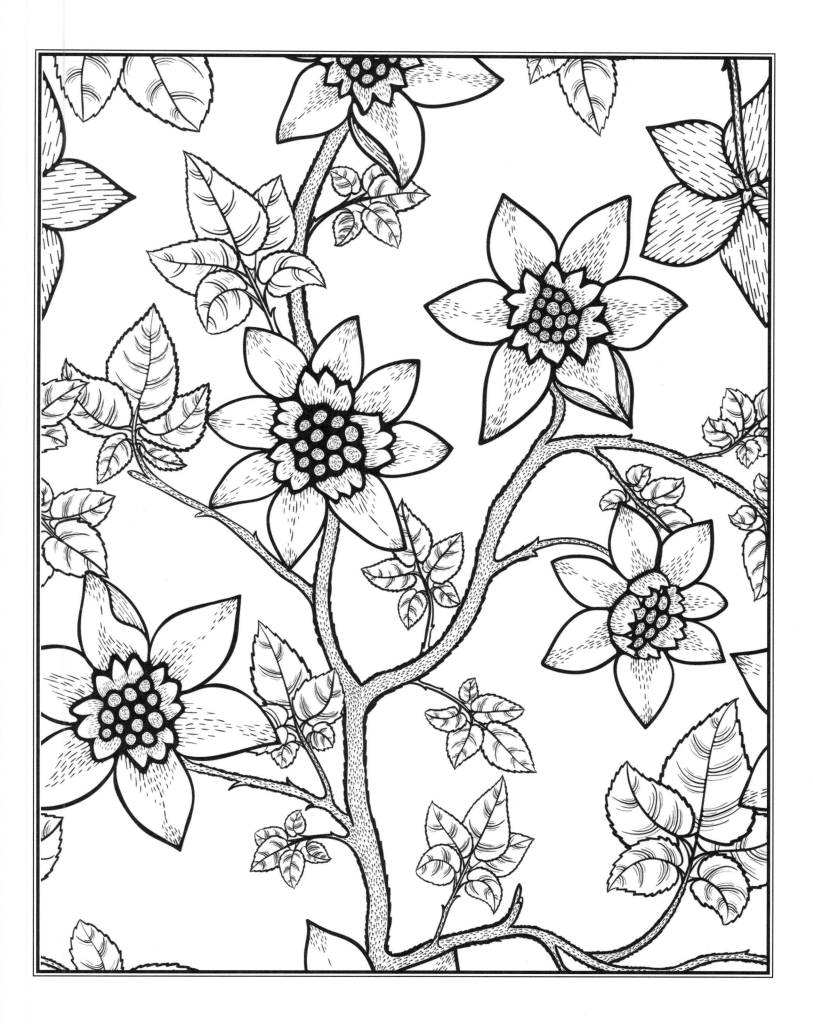